Contents

GONE FISHING

THIS is a book about fishing. It is also a book about life, the life that surrounds us whenever we take a trip to the fresh-waterside or tread the sand and shingle shores of the British Isles.

These pages are intended for the new-comer to the sport of angling, whether young or old in years. It is a fascinating pastime that can rapidly become a way of life. For a fisherman, or woman, does not only become acutely aware of the natural history of his surroundings . . . there is a therapy in fishing. For a few brief hours one's mind is drawn from the worries of life and the speed of modern living to a pace set by nature. For the way in which fishing is conducted and the excitement of it, is dictated by the fish and not by the man holding the rod.

True we can use a superior intellect to outwit the quarry, to encourage them to feed on offerings that could never be re-garded as natural to any wild animal. But, inevitably, it is the fish that makes the decision to co-operate. Success, in angling, is a peculiar thing. If you were to ask a cross-section of fishermen how they measured success in their fishing effort, I am sure that you would get a wide variety of replies. To a lot of people achievement can only be measured in the number of fish landed or the all-in weight of their catch. To others, perhaps the thinking anglers, satisfaction comes with just the odd fish so often that was difficult to catch!

It is possible to enjoy a fishless day, but really only possible when you know, or think you know, why the fish had the beating of you. Anglers rarely return to their homes in a gloomy frame of mind . . . they are too busy planning the next trip to the river or coast.

Never get too serious about the sport, give yourself time to look at the day and remember that fishing is supposed to give pleasure.

Consider the needs and enjoyment of others, observe the Code of the Country-side and you will find that you are wel-come at the waterside.

Michael Prichard
Upminster 1972

Chapter 1
An introduction to freshwater: environment and species

MILLIONS of years ago primitive man decided to forsake the life of a vegetarian and become a flesh eater. Undoubtedly his first item of fishing tackle was the spear. Being of wood with a point roughly shaped with a flint and hardened by fire, this allowed him to fish in depths of water that his spear could be driven down into. Watching fish dart away into the security of the deeper water, no doubt set in motion thoughts of fishing with a weapon that could follow the prey. Using the small right-angled bones gleaned from a previous meal and twisting grasses and sinews gave him a line and hook with which to present a morsel of that meal, and so angling was born.

Although fishing is today a major sport, for both children and adults alike, it is only a sophisticated number of variations of what it was in those far off days. The same rules apply, the rigs and tackles that are used should be simple in design and uncomplicated in use, for they are intended to deceive the fish and not to please the maker. The principal object of any fishing method should be to present what is usually a most unlifelike offering in such a fashion that any fish seeing it will take it without giving the unnatural appearance of the bait a second thought. This coupled with an appreciation of the natural history of fishes and the environment in which they live will enable the newcomer to the sport to get the maximum pleasure from what he is doing.

It has been said that fishing is a thing of the mind, that the satisfaction gained by the angler is a purely personal thing. Certainly this satisfaction is hard to describe to other people for a good day's fishing depends on so many things. Just to hook and land fish is not enough. One must feel for the countryside and be aware of all the life that surrounds the river or pond. In short . . . become the "Compleat Angler".

Let us consider some of the habitats in which we will find fish. For these animals are extremely tolerant of vastly differing conditions of water purity, speed of current, pollutants, oxygen availability and food. I suppose the first kind of habitat, that comes to mind, is the traditional pond. Small in size and so often neglected, it produces small fish: rudd, roach and that love of all small boys, perch. Too often there is insufficient food available to support large fish in any reasonable numbers. Occasionally larger members of the carp family, introduced mirror carp and tench, will grow to large sizes in the small pond but it is unlikely that anything startling will be brought to the angler's net. Gravel pits and other man-made lakes generally produce better catches. Larger in water area, and deeper, they tend to grow bigger specimens. These waters seem to gather less debris. The water is cleaner and clearer which allows the sunlight to penetrate the depths encouraging a more prolific growth of waterplants. These plants, in turn, provide refuge and food for the multitudes of below-surface living animal and insect life. They also assist in the continuous 5

A small pond with little food availability. It can contain a few good fish but is more likely to hold a multitude of small ones that will not grow to any size.

The man-made fishery, a gravel pit in the south of Essex (below). Part of a naturalised gravel pit in Cambridgeshire (below right). Surrounded by trees, the water is rich in animal life and supports large numbers of specimen-size fish.

process of oxygenating the surrounding water for it is through this function together with the ingress of oxygen from the atmosphere that fish and other animals are able to live below the surface of the water. The deep water of ponds and lakes of this type is less affected by changes in air temperature, can hold more oxygen because the water is cooler and altogether will provide more stable conditions for the support of aquatic life.

Fish will not be found spread throughout a large lake or gravel pit; all species will have a pattern of movement from place to place. Their movements are determined by the behavioural urge which is upon them at that moment in time. For example, the carp will spend most of their time rooting in the mud and silt in the deeper parts of the lake. But, depending on conditions of light and temperature, they will move into the shallows to feed on life in the reeded margins. The urge to breed will send them to the

cleaner shallow areas where they spawn over gravel. A warm sunny day may find these fish with their backs out of the water lying motionless among the lily pads. Most animals have a certain number of fixed behaviour patterns and the successful angler is normally the man that has taken considerable trouble to study this routine.

There is another type of still-water situation, the canal. During the Industrial Revolution much of the Midlands and North of Britain was connected by a system of waterways allowing the movement of heavy loads by slow-moving barges. The canals were cut to a standardised width and depth and were ideal for fish and fishing—had they remained as they were built! Unfortunately with the coming of railways most of the canals fell into disuse. They became silted up, choked with uncontrolled weeds and dumping grounds for vast quantities of rubbish. Today, however, the situation is

improving rapidly, for with the ever increasing demand for water areas for recreational purposes there has been a move to re-establish the canal systems. It appears to be the intention of the Government to open these canals to boating, fishing and as a means of transferring water, in bulk, from one area of the country to another. The species of fish found in canals are fewer in number than would be met with in a free-flowing river, basically because there is little if any flow on these waters. They can almost be said to be a long pond, so one expects to find stillwater species predominating.

Small streams and rivers form the largest part of available water for anglers in Britain. They contain the widest variety of species but also are subjected to the greatest number of pressures upon the use of the water for reasons other than angling. Pollution is the biggest single problem. So many of our rivers are regarded as a means of disposing of unwanted domestic and industrial effluents, sewage, unwanted rainfall and just plain rubbish. Agricultural products, fertiliser and pesticides coupled with our most efficient system of land drainage are probably the most serious of the pollutants. When rain falls, it drains through the soil and into the tile drains, quickly swells the small streams then gushes out into our rivers and flushes to the sea. Such chemicals as are in the soil are flushed in massive concentration out into the river systems. There is a lack of continuous flow, as we had in the days before efficient land drainage, which dilutes the chemicals and ensures that they disperse in small doses that fish and other waterlife can tolerate.

This drainage brings yet another problem, for in the drier months we need the water so hurriedly sent into the sea. Then the same people responsible for the winter outflow have to then abstract water from rivers which are flowing at

Lough Ennel (below, left), a huge open water well known as a trout fishery. Lakes of this size often hold numbers of coarse fish, but due to the huge area of the water they are sometimes hard to locate. Canals can provide fair fishing in almost stillwater conditions. They are deep and rarely suffer from water shortage in times of drought.

summer levels . . . a time when the river can least afford to provide for a heavy demand.

It may appear that I have painted a rather gloomy picture of our water resources from an angler's point of view. I believe that it is necessary to realise the importance of the supply of clean and abundant water to both angler and fish alike and to respect the needs of both. Happily most fishermen know that the answer to preserving their waters is to support the national organisations that are constantly pressing the angler's case. Also, it is desirable that all people, of this world, should be aware of the need to provide clean water resources for themselves and future generations.

A small stream (left) full of rushes, weed and fallen tree branches. It may be difficult to fish in summer but becomes easier as the weed dies down at the back end of the year. A slow-running river, meandering through lush water meadows (below, left). This water holds a good head of roach, dace, bream and perch. The River Lune, a fast-flowing salmon and trout water (below), flowing from the moors of Westmorland to the sea at Morecambe. The angler, Brian Harris, is into a salmon in the deep streamy water below the groyne.

Species

Now, we will look at the species of fish that are found in the waters of this country. It may help you to study the illustration (fig. 1) which shows the external anatomical features of most of our freshwater fishes. The position of fins, shape of the body and coloration are most important in the accurate identification of your catch.

I will ignore the very small fry that are not of real angling importance though some may be mentioned where they are used as bait for catching larger species.

Where there are species that look alike, more particularly from a shape point of view, the differences are illustrated by a line drawing. ▶

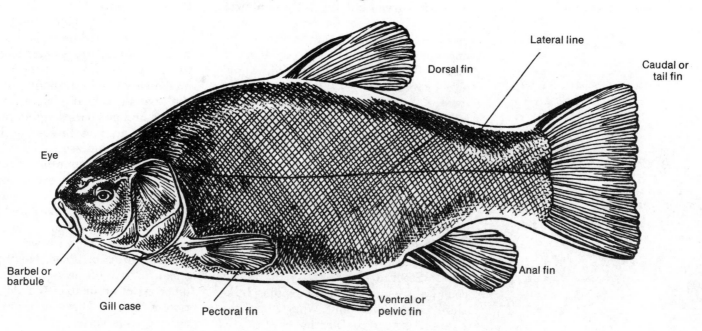

Lateral line

Dorsal fin

Caudal or tail fin

Eye

Barbel or barbule

Gill case

Pectoral fin

Ventral or pelvic fin

Anal fin

Barbel

Barbel *Barbus barbus*

A fish of long slender shape, the back is gently curved but the belly is almost straight. The barbel possesses four barbels, two protruding from the front of the upper jaw and one from each corner of the mouth. The mouth is tube shaped, admirable for rooting in the gravelly bottom for its food. Colour varies from river to river but generally the back is dark olive green which fades to cream on the underside. The fins and tail are large and the scales are very small.

The barbel was formerly a fish of the South and East of England, but was introduced to many other river systems. They seem to live and grow well in clean, fast, unpolluted water. The Severn, Thames, Kennet, Hampshire Avon and Dorset Stour are the best of the South country streams whilst the Swale, Yorkshire Ouse, Nidd and Wharfe are the rivers to visit in the North.

Search out swims with clean gravel bottoms, among rafts of thick weed. Fish with bread baits, cheese, sausage, worms or maggots, they are all good baits to suit this fish's huge appetite.

Bleak *Alburnus alburnus*

A small greeny-coloured fish with silver sides, looking very much like a miniature dace. It is normally 3-6 inches long. It is most often found in the slow-moving rivers of Southern England where it swims in large shoals. Cursed by anglers, when it takes baits intended for larger species, it can be used as a livebait when fishing for perch or pike.

Bream — Bronze *Abramis brama*

This fish has a flat, deep body and is often likened to a dinner plate. The mouth, which is small, stops short at a point in front of the eye. Colour is olive or brownish-green in the adult but silvery in the juvenile fish. Its dorsal fin is placed on the humped back roughly midway between the eye and the start of the tail fin.

Bronze bream are fished for in ponds, lakes and slow-running rivers where there is a prolific weed growth. Seek deepish waters in the South and Midlands of England or the lakes and rivers of Ireland. Bream, which are a shoal fish, are best fished for with worms, maggots and all forms of bread. Having found a shoal, it is often necessary to feed large amounts of groundbait to hold the attention of the fish. They can be shy biters, so carry a wide variety of baits.

Bream—Silver *Blicca bjoernka*

A smaller fish than the bronze bream, it grows to a maximum of 2-3 lbs. Most specimens will not exceed 10-12 ounces, and at this weight they are easily mistaken for the young of the bronze variety.

They are not specifically fished for and can be found in rivers and lakes of Eastern England.

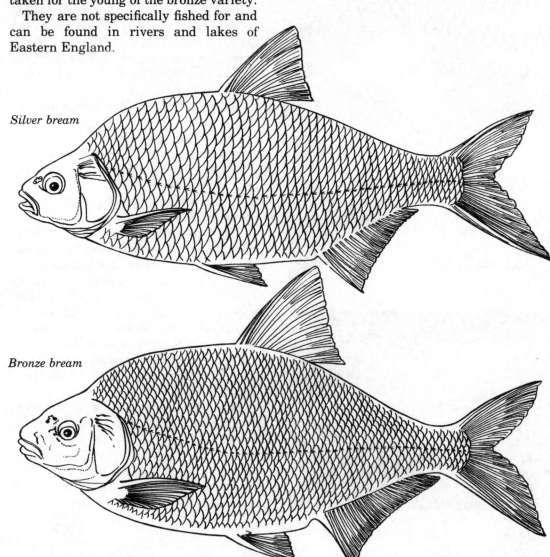

Silver bream

Bronze bream

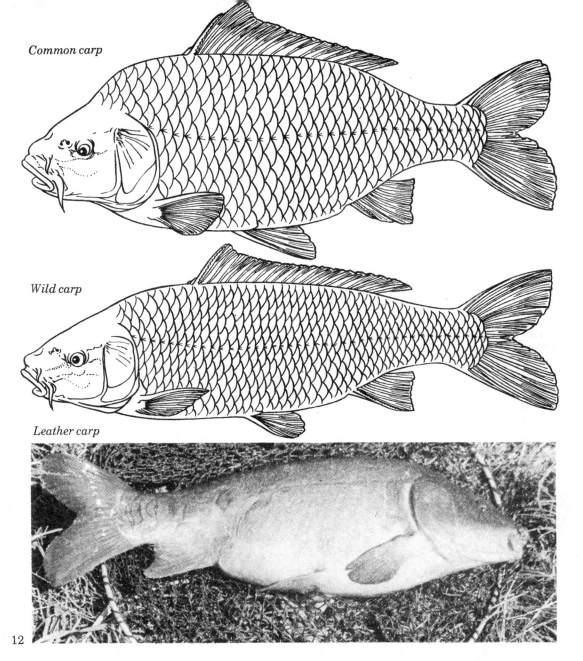

Common carp

Wild carp

Leather carp

Carp *Cyprinus carpio*

There are three varieties of this large species, common, mirror and leather. A deep-bodied, heavy set fish with a long dorsal fin, the carp shows a wide variety of coloration. In the fully-scaled fish the back is a rich purple changing to bronze on its sides and fading to a cream on the belly. Similar colours predominate in the mirror or semi-scaled fish whilst the leather carp is often paler in colour and of course has no scales.

All three varieties have four barbels, two in the middle of the upper jaw and one in the corner, each side of the mouth. There are no teeth in the mouth but the fish has strong throat teeth on the pharyngeal bones. These are probably used to crush crustaceans and other pond life on which the fish feeds.

Carp are widely distributed in British waters, mainly because man has stocked many ponds, lakes and slow-moving rivers with this wild fighter. The species is kept on the Continent to provide food and it is possible that some of our fish originate from stockponds or stews as these fish farms of old were called.

Favourite baits vary from water to water, but certainly bread fished as flake, crust or dough is as good as any. Lob-worms, bunches of maggots and even partly-boiled potatoes are often successful lures.

Crucian carp *Carassius carassius*

Much smaller than the common carp, this fish lacks barbels at the mouth and looks rather like a plump goldfish. It is fully scaled and deep in the body. Bronze-green on the back, it has a small mouth in a rather blunt snout. Size alone will separate this fish from its larger cousin, it rarely grows above a couple of pounds where the mirror carp reaches huge weights of thirty to forty pounds.

Crucians are not widespread in habitat, they are usually found in lakes and ponds of the East and South of the British Isles. Small baits are the order of the fishing day, worms and bread but maggots are really best.

Chub *Squalius cephalus*

A heavy, solid fish often referred to as loggerhead, possibly because it is so thick-shouldered and unmovable. As a young fish is often confused with the dace. It is dark green on the back, changing to bronze on the flanks with a creamy-white belly. The snout is blunt and the mouth large, slightly curved downwards at the corners. The chub's paired fins are pinkish and there may be a faint tinge of pink on the dorsal and tail fin, which also has a dark band on its edge.

This fish is normally found in running water, although some have been introduced with success into stillwater. Look for undercut river banks with overhanging trees and bushes, the shadows cast suit the secretive nature of this fish and a great amount of the fish's food will drop from the vegetation. This fish is noted for taking up residence in a favourite lie, it will be seen in the same spot day after

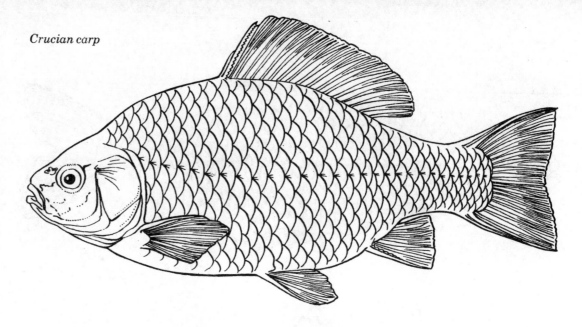

Crucian carp

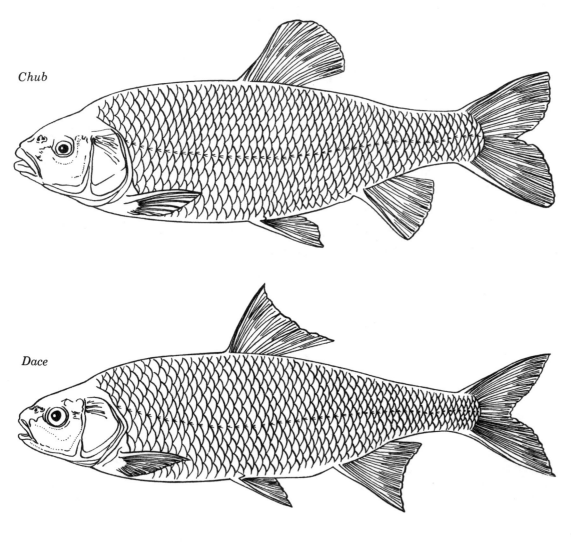

Chub

Dace

day. It is also renowned for dashing into a tree root or impenetrable underwater obstruction when hooked, so strong gear is usual. The chub is fairly widespread in Britain but is absent from the North of Scotland and Cornwall. Recently it has become established, in a small way, in Ireland.

Baits are legion, worms, grubs, slugs, snails, caterpillars, maggots, cheese, bread, small fish, spinning lures and even artificial flies will all tempt the chub. But beware, it is an extremely wary fish and will slink off at the slightest noise of heavy footfalls on the bankside!

Dace *Leuciscus Leuciscus*

Much smaller than the chub, delicate and streamlined, the dace can be identified by its concave dorsal and anal fins. Those of the chub are convex in shape. The dace is silver in colour with a bluish back and greenish fins. The ventral and anal fins are often tinged with pink.

It is a shoal fish that lives in clear, running water and is often seen playing over gravelly shallows. Trotting techniques will catch these little fish and they can also be taken fishing small wet flies. Dace inhabit fast flowing rivers in most of England and across the border into Wales.

Most forms of bread and maggots will take them but be quick on the strike.

Eel *Anguilla anguilla*

This fish starts life in saltwater. Spawned in the Sargasso Sea it spends

14

several years floating on its journey to the rivers of Britain. Arriving as a minute elver, it ascends the rivers and streams into the tiniest brook and even into land-locked pools to feed and grow to maturity. After a number of years residing in our waters it will make its way to the sea once more and swim south to the Atlantic spawning grounds, to breed and to die. The eel is easily recognised, just two fins both of which extend almost the full length of the body. When young it is silver in colour, changing when adult to dark brown on the back and yellow on the underside.

Found in practically every stretch of freshwater, it is best fished for at night with a legered dead fish or lobworm. Strong tackle is a must for this fish, it is incredibly rugged, dour in the fight and hard to kill. Most eel fishers use a quick-release trace which they disengage from the reel line and then quickly drop the eel into a sack. The hooks are re-covered later after recasting with another trace and bait.

Grayling *Thymallus thymallus*

Beautifully formed silvery-blue scales mark this fish. A large dorsal fin and a small fleshy adipose fin, in front of the tail, show it to be a member of the salmon family. Found in fast streams of the North of England and in Scotland, although some rivers of the South hold a fair head, it will accept baits close to its natural food, namely, worms, insects and maggots.

The grayling can be caught fly fishing

or, in the winter, trotting small worms down the stream on light roach or dace tackle. It puts up a strong fight in fast flows and is traditionally sought after in the autumn when the trout season has closed.

Gudgeon *Gobio gobio*

Another of the smaller fishes often used as livebait for perch and pike. Look-ing like a miniature barbel, though they have only two barbels, these little chaps are dark brown in colour with blotches on the sides and disproportionately large scales. Found in most of Britain except Scotland.

Perch *Perca fluviatilis*

Unmistakable in colour and shape, this striking fish has two dorsal fins. The first with about fourteen sharp spines and a dark patch at the rear, the second with

Perch

15

two short, stiff spines and fourteen or so soft rays. The back in most fish is olive green in colour with yellow flanks and a white belly. Several dark stripes, in a vertical pattern, give a camouflage effect to the sides of this freshwater predator.

The fins and tail are pink and grow brighter in the breeding season. This species favours slow-running rivers and stillwater, where it lurks in deep holes and close under the banksides. Widespread in the British Isles, but rarely seen in Scotland. Can be fished for with deadbait, but is best baited for with live worms, maggots, insects and small fish. Perch will take spun lures, but of the smaller sizes.

Pike *Esox lucius*

Found in all waters throughout the country, this fish has earned the reputation of being a killer. Undoubtedly it is responsible for the deaths of many fine fish but it is also one of Nature's dustbin-men. As a scavenger it has no equal. Long, sleek and ferocious it spends much time hiding to ambush from weed cover where its colour, a yellow and green marbling, blends in with the surrounding vegetation. The dorsal and anal fins are almost at the back of the body and the mouth, with its extended bottom jaw, is large.

In the wild the Pike will kill fish, animals such as rats and voles, water birds and small invertebrate life. We can fish almost any bait that moves or looks at all lifelike. Spinners and plugs, of metal and wood, live fish or a legered dead fish. Sometimes pike fishing can be slow; there is a theory that these predators have an enormous meal then lie around in a placid state for days before coming on to feed once more.

Pike perch or Zander *Lucioperca lucioperca*

This species may possess some of the characteristics of the pike and perch but is not a hybrid between the two. It is a separate species which was introduced to this country from eastern Europe. Is long and sleek with two dorsal fins, the first having spikes, the other is soft and rayed. The fish is dark green on its back with lighter flanks and has broad, dark vertical bars on each side. Zander are only found in a few river systems in East Anglia and a couple of lakes in the Home Counties.

As with the perch and pike, this fish takes bait or artificial spinning lures.

Pike

16

Roach *Rutilus rutilus*

It is probable that more anglers fish for roach than any other species. They are found almost everywhere in widely differing habitats. They are unfortunately absent from the North of Scotland but can be had in two Irish river systems. This species is often mistaken for the rudd, a similar member of the carp family. The illustration shows the main identification points of the two fish.

Roach are a dark greenish black on the back, shading to silver flanks and a white underside. The dorsal fin has a concave edge and is placed directly over the ventral fins. All seven fins have a pinkish tinge which brightens at the breeding period.

Roach will take a variety of hook-baits, worms, maggots, all forms of bread bait, grubs, wheat and hemp. They are not a large fish, a pound roach is an average specimen for most waters.

Rudd *Scardinius erythrophthalmus*

Deeper in the body than the roach, with similar colouring but more golden on the sides. The fins are pink of a brighter hue. The dorsal fin is placed further to the rear of the fish, behind the ventrals. The eyes of this species are a brilliant red and the bottom jaw extends beyond the top.

Found all over the country except in Scotland, this fish is particularly common in Ireland *(where it is often called roach)*. It is mainly confined to slow-running rivers and stillwater pools.

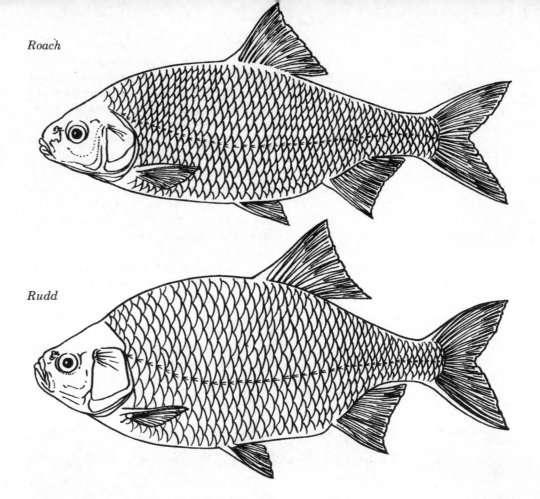

Roach

Rudd

It will accept the same baits as the roach but also takes the fly quite freely on warm summer evenings.

Salmon *Salmo salar*

A fish of the sea and the rivers. It begins life in the upper reaches of a number of clean, swift-flowing streams. Spending up to three years growing in the river,

17

when it is known as a parr, it then moves down to the sea. At this stage it is called a smolt and takes on a silvery scaling. The salmon then goes to sea and lives and feeds in the depths of the Atlantic Ocean. Upon its return, as a fish of from four to fifty pounds, it will make its way up into the river in which it was spawned to start another generation. Having spawned it is in poor condition and is known as a kelt. It often dies in the effort to regain the saltwater. Some fish, however, will make the spawning journey several times during their lives.

This king of fish does not feed when returning to spawn. It will, fortunately for us, take an artificial fly or spinner, though why this is we do not know.

Seek clean unpolluted rivers with a fairly good flow. Ask around among the local fishermen about known salmon 'lies', places where these fish stop to rest on their journeying. Fish with spinning lures, bar spoons or artificial flies.

Salmon

Tench *Tinca tinca*

A close relative of the carp, the tench is bronze-green in colour with large rounded fins. It has minute scales which are embedded in the skin. There is a small barbule at each corner of the down-curved mouth. The fish has extremely small red eyes and can be very slimy to the touch.

Found in a wide variety of ponds, lakes and in a few slow-moving rivers it likes to root around in the mud for the minute organisms that form its natural diet. The tench is absent from the North of Scotland but dwells in all other parts of the British Isles. It is a fish of summer, traditionally fished for on the first day of the coarse fishing season. Tench fishing almost ceases in the late autumn, when this species hibernates in the mud at the bottom of the lake or river.

Use the lift-float method or leger the deep water with worm, bread or a bunch of maggots.

Trout—Brown *Salmo trutta*

A fish of the salmon family and widespread in distribution. Kept in man-made reservoirs, lakes and ponds as well as rivers and streams. I say kept because this fish is often bred artificially, reared and released into many environments. This is the quarry of the bulk of fly fishermen and a wonderful fighter it can be.

Colour varies from water to water and even one part of a river to the next. Generally the fish is dark brown or greeny-brown on the back. Silver on the sides and belly with dark spots over the sides and back. Along the lateral line and either side of it there are a number of red spots, often with white rings around them. Trout have a long slender body with an adipose fin, small and fleshy, between the dorsal and the tail.

They have a huge appetite and will take all forms of minute waterlife. Trout are great predators on the young of their own kind. Fish with spinners if these are allowed as an angling method or fly fish. At times worms will be a killing bait and you will often find them taking maggots intended for coarse fish.

Trout — Rainbow *Salmo irideus*

This fish is similar in shape to the brown trout although it varies in colour. Along its flanks there is a band of purple-reddish speckling which gives the fish its name. It is not as widespread as the native brown trout having been introduced to the continent of Europe from the United States.

Trout — Sea *Salmo trutta*

The same species as the brown trout but a fish that elects to go to sea for the rich feeding that it can find there. It is spawned, like the salmon, in freshwater, grows in the river and then leaves to reach maturity in saltwater. It returns to breed in the headwaters of our rivers, which are usually the clean, fast-water streams. Can be fished for in the same way as brown trout, but being often larger it requires stronger tackle.

Tench

A brown trout with four rainbow trout

19

Chapter 2
Coarse fishing: tackle and baits

PROBABLY the most widely used method for angling in fresh water. Basically the float does two things; it provides a way in which a bite from a taking fish can be detected and is used as a means of supporting or suspending a bait. Conditions prevailing in running or still water will determine which of the methods of fishing should be considered. There is quite a variation in technique for the many rivers and it is important to be able to choose the correct style that will take fish.

Rods

There are literally hundreds of designs in a number of different materials. For many years split cane and combinations of this material with whole cane and greenheart were the basic rod-building materials. Then came solid glass fibre — a useful substitute but far too heavy for coarse fishing rods. Certainly it could not easily be broken but lacked that essential steeliness so necessary when building striking action into a rod. Hollow steel tubular rods came along and very good some of them were and still are but it was with the arrival of hollow-fibre-glass tubes that fishing rods took on a new and exciting pattern. Here was an immensely strong material, light in weight, steely in action and relatively cheap to produce. Hollow glass rods have almost entirely taken over in the coarse fishing world.

My choice of rods to cover all of the fishing situations that I involve myself in would be: a 'general purpose', all

action type of the kind that was evolved to fish the River Avon, in Hampshire, and indeed so often bears the name Avon. About twelve feet in length, with a fairly fast striking tip but progressive action right through to the butt. Used with 2½-4 lbs. line, a fixed-spool reel and float tackle it would suit delicate fishing for roach and dace and yet be equally at home landing a good sized tench or chub. This rod because of its length and progressive action would be ideal for trotting a river or float fishing at distance in still water. It has the power to pick up line over long distances and also set a hook effectively.

Match fishing demands a different action in the rod, anything from twelve to fifteen feet long, only the top eighteen inches or so has flexibility. Designed for extreme speed in the strike, it will be used on slow-running rivers and still-waters to take small fish.

For a long time leger rods were short stiff affairs, totally unsuited to this fine art. Then a Hertfordshire man, Richard Walker, changed the entire legering scene. He produced, in cane, the now famous Mark IV series of rods. Although the Mark IV Avon was really intended for float fishing in the Avon style it became an exceptional legering tool. The most famous of his rods is undoubtedly the Mark IV Carp. Here the accent is on a powerful rod capable of landing the heaviest and strongest of fish, whilst at the same time still retaining the ability to cast light baits for long distances.

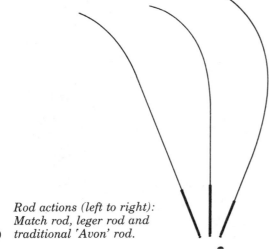

Rod actions (left to right): Match rod, leger rod and traditional 'Avon' rod.

Today these rods have been almost duplicated in their actions by building in fibre glass. Many designers and manufacturers of rods have introduced a great number of their products based on Richard Walker's originals, most are very good indeed but few have quite the subtlety of their cane predecessors.

It is all important that coarse fishing rods should carry rings of the correct type. Stand-off rings on the Avon and match rods will keep light lines away from the glass blank (fig. 1). Lines, otherwise, would tend to stick to the rod surface when casting, especially when the atmosphere is damp, so shortening the cast. This point is not so important with leger rods for the heavier species, as here casting weight tends to overcome the tendency of monofilament line to stick to the rod.

A fully corked handle about two feet long on all three rods will ensure a perfect grip at the reel with the handle lying nicely under the forearm. Hollow glass tube has made a radical improvement in the method of joining rod sections together. There is now no need to use ferrules which add weight and blank off part of the flexing action of the entire rod. Solid or hollow glass spigots (fig. 2) can be used to provide a joint of more than adequate strength.

There are two further rods that I find useful, both are spinning rods and again are made of hollow glass fibre tube. The lighter of the pair is for perch and trout spinning, is eight feet long and has a sweet action right through to the butt. Used with lines of about 3-5 lbs. B/S, the rod will cast a light spinner good distances and yet have enough guts to land a hard-fighting fish. The companion to this spinner is a ten-feet rod, similar in action and design but with more power for salmon or pike.

Both have good quality rings suitable for constant casting, with large breaker rings at the butt. This type of ring aids casting as it smooths out the coils of line as they peel off from a fixed spool reel. There is no real reason why a small freshwater multiplier could not be used with either of these rods. Certainly there is an advantage in using such a reel when salmon spinning. It is able to throw larger lures and is more accurate when dropping a lure on a chosen spot. This is because the free spool of a multiplying reel is easier to control with the thumb. A number of salmon spinners prefer to use braided Terylene lines, they do not stretch under pressure and can only be cast well from a reel of this kind.

Reels

The fixed spool (fig. 3) is the maid of all work to freshwater fishers. The inventor of this reel, A. Holden-Illingworth of Bradford, patented his design in 1905. He was involved in the textile industry and must surely have got the idea for the reel's operation from the bobbins used to carry thread. The present day fixed spool varies little from Illingworth's reel. The line is picked up by a bale arm which

Fig. 1

*A stand-off ring for
float fishing rods.*

Fig. 2

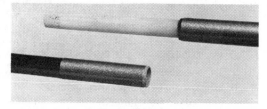

*A solid glass spigot ferrule. Providing that
the hollow glass tube is adequately reinforced
by whipping both end sections, this form of
joint is both strong and cuts weight in the rod.
Spigot joints, in solid or hollow glass, preserve
the natural curve of the rod under compression.*

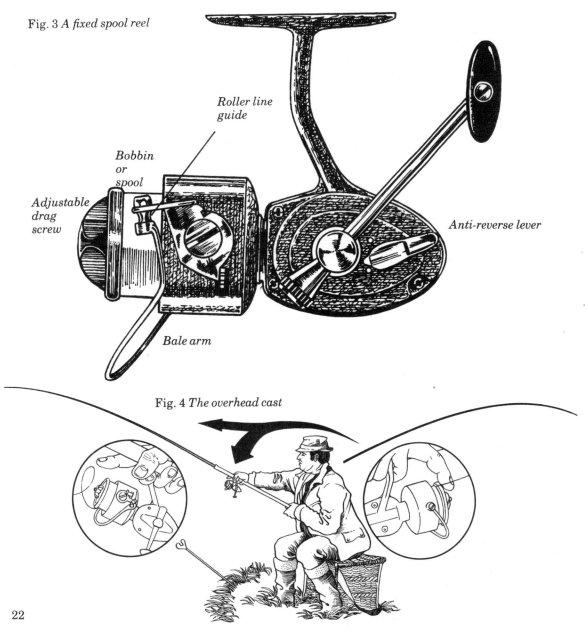

Fig. 3 *A fixed spool reel*

Roller line guide

Bobbin or spool

Adjustable drag screw

Anti-reverse lever

Bale arm

Fig. 4 *The overhead cast*

revolves around a stationary bobbin. Each time the handle of the reel is turned a number of winds of line are made. At the same time the bobbin moves forwards and backwards along the axis of the rod, smoothly laying the coils along the entire length of the spool.

To cast (fig. 4) the line is picked up from the spool with the index finger (some anglers prefer to jam the nylon on the rim of the bobbin instead). The bale arm is folded down on its hinge and locked. Swing the rod back over the shoulder and then forward smartly. At the moment of maximum forward thrust the index finger is straightened allowing the line to peel off the bobbin. The line can be arrested, during flight of the tackle, by jamming the index finger down onto the rim of the spool. Immediately after casting the bale arm is closed by winding the handle of the reel.

The main drawback to this popular type of reel is that there is a considerable loss of distance in the cast due to line friction over the lip of the bobbin. This can be cut down by filling the spool correctly to the point shown (fig. 5). Friction is also present when winding the line back onto the spool. Obviously there is considerable drag caused by line pulling through the rod rings but it is the dragging of line through a right angle at the bale arm that can weaken the line. Use a reel with a free-running roller in the bale arm and ensure that the roller does, in fact, turn under pressure. A few minutes' attention to cleaning this after the fishing day will prevent sudden line breakage.

On most reels there is a clutch mechanism on the front face of the bobbin. This is best adjusted to the breaking strain of the line before fishing commences but additional stopping power can always be applied by placing a finger on the rim of the spool. It is wise to have a number of spare spools for the reel, carrying different breaking strains of line.

The fishing line

Today there is only really one type of line used for float and leger angling: monofilament nylon which is made from synthetic polymeric amide, a material which when formed as a continuous strand is as strong as mild steel of the same gauge. It can be said to be waterproof and has only one failing when used for fishing: nylon line can, and does, lose strength without warning. The answer to this problem is never to keep line on a reel for too long; after all it is reasonably cheap and suffers much abuse during its fishing life.

Knots for nylon

A good knot, in nylon, should possess three properties. It must be strong and perform the function for which it has been tied and be simple to tie. Cold weather and frozen fingers will soon prove the value of the last qualification.

Three knots cover most of the coarse fisherman's needs.

The tucked half-blood knot (fig. 6) is ideal for the attachment of swivels and eyed hooks to nylon. It is probably the finest knot for preserving the maximum strength of the line, quoted by manufacturers as being 85% of the breaking strain. To tie it, pass the line through the eye of the swivel or hook and twist it back over the main line four times. Then pass the free end through the first twist formed and back through the large loop to tuck it. Lick the loose turns to lubricate the nylon and allow the coils to slip along the main line. Now pull tight.

To join two lines together use the double-blood knot (fig. 7). It is the best method of tying lines together as the knot will not slip even when joining lines of unequal thickness and breaking strains. Begin by wrapping one of the free ends around the other line four times, then pass the end of the line, used for forming the coils, between the strands. Hold the coils between the thumb and forefinger to prevent them unwinding. Take up the other free end of line and wrap it around its neighbour four times but in the opposite direction. Finally pass the end

Fig. 5 *Spool loading*

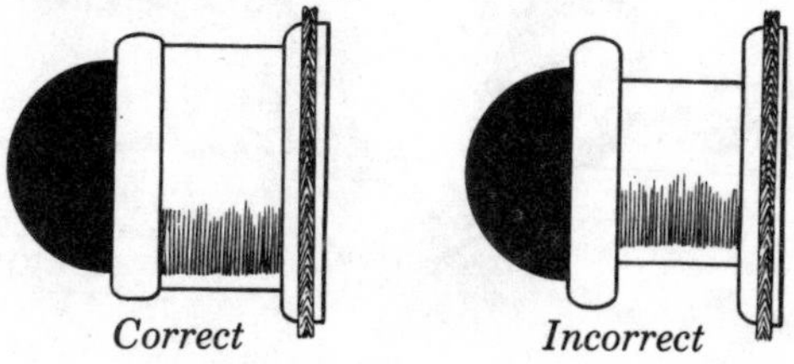

Correct   *Incorrect*

Fig. 6 *Tucked half-blood knot*

Fig. 7 *Double-blood knot*

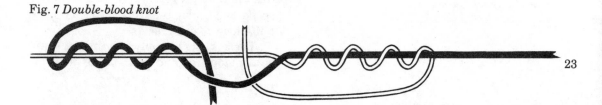

23

Fig. 8 *The figure-of-eight knot, used to form a loop in a hook snood.*

through the centre loop, lick and pull gently on both lines. If the two strands are of vastly differing dimensions it may be necessary to seat the coils by easing them into place with your fingernails.

To attach hook snoods or paternoster traces to the reel line use the simple and efficient figure-of-eight knot. Again it is an extremely strong knot of about 75% line strength (fig. 8).

There is another knot for attaching a hook to nylon and is most often used to tie on the spade-end variety of hook. These are hooks that have no eyes but rely on a swelling at the top of the hook shank preventing coils of nylon which are whipped around the shank from slipping off (fig. 9). Hold the hook in the thumb and first finger of the left hand, take the free end of line and pinch a loop with the same thumb and finger. Try to give yourself a free end of about five inches. With the right hand wrap six turns of nylon around the shank of the hook — at the same time keeping the coils fairly tight. Then pass the free end of the line through the large loop which was held in the left hand, whilst maintaining tension on the coils. Slowly draw the main line tight, this will close the loop and tighten the coils. Further pulling on the line will draw the knot along the shank of your hook and effectively secure the knot. If properly tied this knot, for spade-end hooks, is as reliable as a tucked half-blood to eyed hooks.

These knots are only suitable for tying with nylon line and must *not* be used for

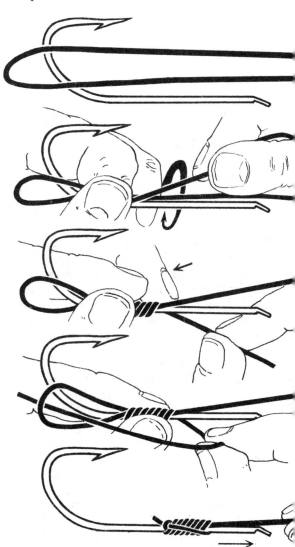

Fig. 9 *A whipping knot for tying nylon to a spade-end hook.*

Terylene or Dacron braided line. These knots tend to strangle the fibres of braided materials thereby drastically reducing the breaking strain of lines, which in turn could result in the loss of good fish!

Hooks

There must be literally hundreds of different hook patterns with almost as many weird and wonderful names for them. Many are suitable for angling purposes but many are not.

The basic requirements in a good hook are few but all are equally important. A hook should be as strong as possible without being excessively thick in the wire from which it is made. It should possess good power of penetration together with adequate holding ability.

The size of hook one should use is dictated by two separate factors, the size of bait and the size of the fish. Some of the most useful patterns are shown in fig. 10 together with a scale of hook sizes. Large fish, such as the carp, would require a good quality hook size 2-6 because a large bread bait or even a bunch of lobworms would be used. Carp are found in British waters up to forty pounds in weight and have tough leathery mouths, so they demand a large hook to provide an adequate hook hold.

Fishing with maggots or casters, on the other hand, for roach would require a fine wire hook of size 12-18, this species averaging 8 ounces to just over a pound in most waters. In all freshwater fishing the hook size must be balanced to the rest

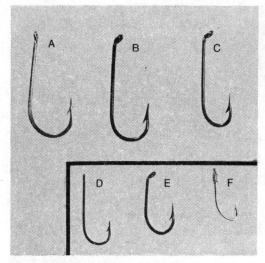

Fig. 10 *Hook patterns for freshwater fishing:*
A. *A brazed eye, forged hook for carp fishing. Short in the point and very strong.*
B. *Long-shanked, round bend with a down-turned eye for all forms of coarse fishing, available in sizes 2-18.*
C. *Kirby hook with a fairly long shank, down eyed and forged.*
D. *Straight eyed, round bend, short in the point and fine in the wire.*
E. *Short-shanked, down-eyed Model Perfect.*
F. *Crystal hook tied to a nylon cast or snood. A very popular hook available in a wide range of sizes 1/0-20.*

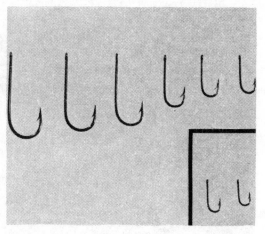

Scale of hook sizes:
Straight-eyed, bronzed and forged freshwater hooks in sizes 4 (largest)—18.

A big humpty-backed bream taken fishing the lift-float method in a gravel pit.

Fig. 11

of the tackle and the species fished for. There would be little point in fishing with two pounds B/S nylon to a size 6 hook as it would be very difficult to drive the hook home on such fine line. Conversely, an 18 hook fished to 6 pound line would probably mean that the hook would tear from the mouth of most fish.

Hooks are available from the tackle shop either tied direct to nylon of a stated breaking strain or loose. Both have their uses, the tied hook for most forms of float fishing and the loose hook where the angler decides to leger, when it is more usual to tie the hook direct to the reel line. It is important to remember one thing, wherever possible have the minimum number of joins and knots in your line. The more joins made—the weaker the connection to your hook becomes.

One form of freshwater fishing demands a trace made of wire and this is fishing either by float or leger for pike.

This fierce predatory species has extremely sharp teeth which can bite clean through most nylon traces. Therefore we make up a wired trace carrying a number of hooks. The illustration (fig. 11) shows how the treble hooks are attached to the wire. The end treble is fixed by twisting the wire back around itself and then a further treble is placed on the trace in such a way as to allow considerable adjustment of its position. Finally, a single hook is placed at the head of the trace to make the tail of the bait secure. This tackle would then be joined to the reel line using a link swivel.

Floats

A float is used for two purposes, firstly, to support the bait at a predetermined depth and, secondly, to give indication of a bite. The float is the key figure in the tackle system. Later in this chapter I will discuss the use of a float allied to particular fishing methods but basically a float fishing rig has a hook carrying the bait, a number of leads to take the bait down to where the fish are feeding (these will vary in number and in size depending on current flow, etc.) and a float capable of supporting the whole.

In the illustration (fig. 12) a few of the many floats available to anglers are shown. 1. A French pike float with extending antennae, used to suspend a live-bait. This type of float presents little resistance to a taking fish, and can be easily seen by the angler at distance.

2. A deep water pike sliding float, the line is passed through a tube in the body of the float and can be adjusted for depth by attaching a stop to the reel line. The same float is often used by sea anglers fishing from rocks or in harbours. 3 and 4. These are typical 'Avon' floats, used when trotting fairly strong rivers where the current has a marked pulling effect on the rig so that a float with good carrying capacity is necessary. 5. A style of trotting float used by Northern anglers when fishing for grayling. It was designed by R. V. Righyni as a self-cocking float and is made of balsa wood with a wire stem. 6. Stick float, used to fish with light tackle on a slow-running river in windy conditions. The float is shotted down in the water so that just the crown of the float is visible presenting little surface to strong wind. 7. A traditional and still

Fig. 12

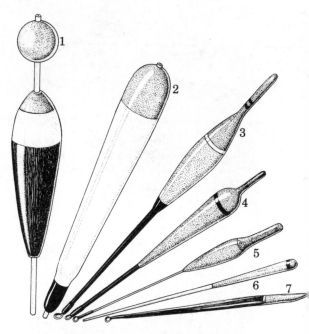

1. *French pike float with extending antennae.*
2. *Deep-water pike or sea sliding plastic float.*
3. *Avon trotting float.*
4. *Avon trotting float.*
5. *R. V. Righyni's grayling self-cocking float.*
6. *Stick float.*
7. *Porcupine quill.*

Float fishing at night or during half-light can produce a headache! Bites registered on the float are almost impossible to detect. After the float has settled direct the beam from a torch onto the float tip. Keep the angle parallel to the water surface, the float will be easily seen and there will be little frightening effect upon the fish.

27

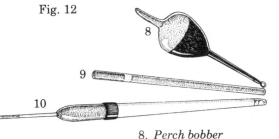

Fig. 12

8. *Perch bobber*
9. *Peacock quill*
10. *Plastic self-cocking float*
11. *'Zuma' long-casting float*
12. *Antennae float*

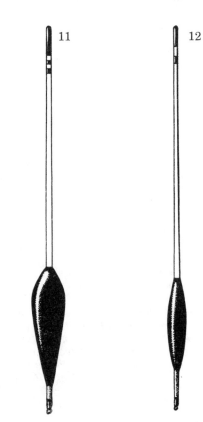

widely used float for general still-water fishing. 8. Another traditional float, used when fishing worms or minnow livebaits to perch. The problem is that this float is poorly shaped and requires quite a pull before it will register a bite. Perch, particularly big ones, are cagey fish and might drop a bait upon feeling the resistance from the float. 9. A first class general float. It can be had made-up or bought as lengths of peacock quill. Float lengths of any size can be cut off and being white the float length only needs varnishing. 10. Another self cocking float, loaded with either lead shot or water to the desired amount to make it ride at the correct level. I have used them to trot a light livebait on a slow moving river for pike and perch. Made in plastic, the float is, of course, hollow. 11. The antennae float, used to beat windy conditions. The bulk of the body is low down on the stem of the float. In a strong wind the line is blown across the water which pulls a float and makes it sink. Attach the antennae at the float bottom only. When the tackle has settled on the bottom place the rod into the rests so that the rod tip is just below the surface of the water. Then tighten the line. This will ensure a tight line under the surface, unaffected by wind, and a mere inch or so of float stick showing. 12. This is a float designed for long distance casting. It has sufficient weight and is of the correct aerodynamic shape to allow a perfect flight through the air. Known as the zoomer, it can be had in a vast range of lengths and weights.

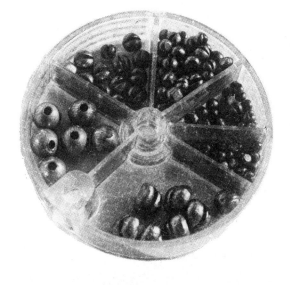

Fig. 14

Split shot   *'Styl' leads*

28

Swivels and leads

Apart from pike fishing, coarse fishing is generally a delicate business so all swivels and associated ironmongery should be kept to the minimum. Certainly they have a use in spinning and sometimes in legering and paternostering but keep them down in size and take care that they do not become rusted or fouled with dirt which will prevent them functioning effectively. Barrel, three-way and link swivels are the most often used (fig. 13) and their purposes will be discussed when dealing with specific rigs and methods.

Leads for coarse fishing are broadly speaking of two types. Those that are pinched onto the line to take a bait down to fish and those that run freely on the line to enable the end tackle to hold bottom. Split shot, which is sliced, comes in a wide range of sizes for pinching onto the line below the float (fig. 14). There is a numbering system which bears a relationship to size, but not weight, of shot as follows: Swan, AAA,BB,1,2,3,4,5,6,8. Swan is largest and 8, or dust shot, smallest. The important thing to know is not the weight of the leads so much as just what leads each of your floats will carry. It is a good idea to spend a little time loading each float before floating them in a bath to arrive at their carrying capacity and then writing the weights onto the body of the float. It may appear to be a fiddly job but it is one which saves valuable fishing time. Another kind of lead for float fishing is the 'Styl' lead. It is useful pinched onto the line in the same way as shot but will not be mouthed by fish used to taking hemp or baits which look very like split shot!

Leger weights are normally made to definite weights, ¼-1 ounce are the best sizes and they come in a number of shapes. Drilled bullets and coffin leads are intended to have the line threaded through them and the bomb lead (fig. 15) which has a swivel at its head, also runs on the reel line. The fourth lead, looking something like a pyramid is in fact a lead plummet used in float fishing to ascertain the depth of water in the angler's swim. The hook is taken through the wire loop and stuck into the cork insert at the base of the lead. The lead is then lowered into the water and the position of the float noted and adjusted accordingly.

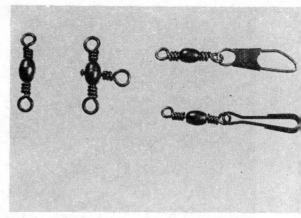

Fig. 13 *Swivels for coarse fishing*

Fig. 15 *Leger weights*

Fig. 16 *Lightweight alloy-framed landing net*

The rest of the tackle

Having bought the rod, reel, line and necessary items to catch a fish what do we do when it is played to the bank? If a very small fish it can be carefully lifted, on the line, and taken from the hook. But let us think of bigger fish. A good landing net is the answer, triangular in shape at the mouth with a handle at least four feet long (fig. 16). If you are after large species then please make certain that the fish will be able to fit into the net. It is heart-breaking to lose any fish at this point.

Conventionally, pike are gaffed. This severely injures the pike although some people talk of chin gaffing being humane. This method relies on the angler being able to accurately insert the hook of the gaff at a point just behind the rim of the jaw. Certainly this method will not harm the fish if done correctly, but I would rather play the pike out and land it in a large net.

It is not always easy to remove the hook from the throat of a fish, so a disgorger should always be carried (fig. 17). This instrument is slipped down the nylon line until it rests against the hook bend; slight downward pressure will push the barb backwards and so release the hook hold. For a fish that has been hooked deep in the throat there are only two alternatives: if not bleeding and in otherwise good condition, a pair of artery forceps can be clamped over the hook and removal made carefully (fig. 18) but if the fish is badly injured the best policy is to kill it humanely.

Fig. 17 *A slotted disgorger*

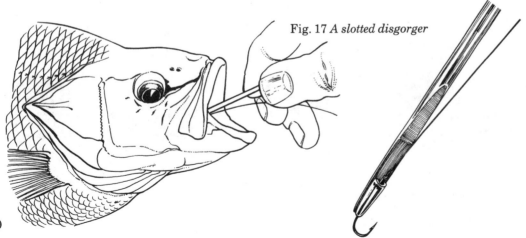

30

Anglers like to keep their catch either to be photographed or to be admired at the end of the day. Indeed it can be a bad thing to return fish to a swim immediately after unhooking, the released fish seems to scuttle back to the shoal and pass the word that something is wrong! So fishermen have keepnets in which to place the fish as they are caught. To be humane in use a keepnet should be at least five feet long, between 15 and 18 inches in diameter and have the net supported at intervals along its length so as not to crush the occupants. Ideally the net should be soft in texture because it is often found that the knots in nylon nets rub the scales from fish. With the scales goes the protective slime and almost immediately the fish is prone to the ingress of waterborne disease. Keepnets that are too small and possibly, at times, overcrowded cause damage and deaths through crushing.

Obviously there are many other items of tackle to be found in the freshwater angler's tackle box. It will be better though to mention their uses as we go on to deal with the specific methods of fishing in still and running water.

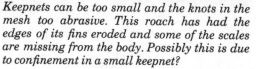

Keepnets can be too small and the knots in the mesh too abrasive. This roach has had the edges of its fins eroded and some of the scales are missing from the body. Possibly this is due to confinement in a small keepnet?

Fig. 18 If a fish is hooked deep in the gullet, artery forceps will grip the shank more positively.

31

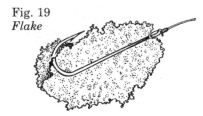

Fig. 19
Flake

Natural baits

Bread. The ordinary household loaf must surely provide more anglers with baits and sport than any other form of offering. If I had to fish with only one type of bait for coarse angling it would be bread. The inside of a stale loaf provides the raw material for making paste. Fresh, a loaf gives two good baits, flake and crust. The illustration (fig. 19) shows how to bait a hook with flake. Tear out a piece from the inside of a fresh loaf and pinch the bread lightly at a point where the hook eye emerges. Do not squeeze the flake onto the hook shank too tightly because when immersed in water the bread will go too hard making it difficult to strike the hook point through to the jaw of the fish. Flake makes first-class slow-sinking bait as it has little weight. It will also fish well over blanket weed or a soft muddy bottom where heavier baits would disappear from sight of the fish.

Crust, torn from the side of a fresh loaf, is a great bait on two counts: it can be made to sink to the bottom by moulding an amount of paste on the underside of the crust or fished as a floating surface bait for fish such as carp. Attach the crust to the hook by piercing the soft flaking underside, taking the hook up and through the crust and then pull the hook point clear on the soft side (fig. 20).

As I said before, paste is best made from the interior of a stale loaf. Begin by pulling out a large piece of flake, dampen with a small amount of water and wrap the bread in a piece of clean cloth. Then

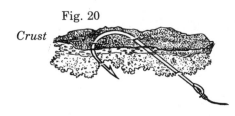

Fig. 20
Crust

squeeze out as much of the water as you can. Knead the bread between the fingers until the paste is of a firm but pliable consistency and avoid a tough, leathery mixture. To be a good bait, paste should just stay on the hook during the cast.

Maggots. Small in size, maggots can be used as a bait to take even the largest of fishes. Carp, barbel, tench and pike have all been caught on this blue-bottle grub. The essential thing to remember when using maggots is to preserve the natural appearance of the bait. These grubs wiggle attractively but only if placed on the hook by gently nicking the flesh with the hook point as in fig. 21. Avoid threading them onto the hook bend where they soon die, lose all movement and cease to attract fish that are in the swim. They can be fished singly on a size 18 hook for dace, or as a bunch on a larger iron for bigger species. A few loose maggots thrown into the swim will act as groundbait and draw fish to your hook-bait.

Worms. Second only to bread, worms of all kinds and sizes will take fish. Large lobworms (fig. 22) fished on a number 8 hook are a wonderful tench bait whilst a bunch of worms will take carp. The only problem is that most species of fish find the worm to their liking so that your carp or tench offering will often be grabbed by an eel or perch. Brandlings are a good trotting bait and can be fished to grayling and other river species. Continental anglers fish with a minute bloodworm (fig. 23); hook sizes must be small, about 22-24, to hold this bait.

Other baits

Many other small creatures can be used as bait, the grubs of wasps, snails, shrimps, slugs, all have their place. Cheese, either as a paste or in chunks will attract chub and on some river systems barbel take sausage meat (fig. 24) eagerly. I suppose that at some time most human foods can catch a fish and it is well worthwhile trying a wide variety of bait especially when the traditional baits are proving fruitless.

It must be realised that all fish, at some time in their lives, are predatory. There are very few freshwater fish that will not take another fish and even the young of their own species as a meal. So we must consider fish to be a bait with many uses. I will deal with the fish baits in those sections of this book where specific methods are discussed.

Groundbait

This is generally made from cereals, finely ground in texture and mixed with water to form a stiff dough. Thrown into a lake or river it is intended to draw fish that may be some distance from your fishing pitch into the swim. Ideally the groundbait should be made of a similar substance to that with which the angler is fishing, for there is very little purpose in drawing fish with cereals and then presenting a maggot or worm hook bait!

Fig. 23 *Bloodworms*

Fig. 24 *Sausage meat*

Fig. 21 *Maggots*

Fig. 22 *Lobworm*

Groundbaiting can take many forms — maggots dribbled constantly into a swim and fished on the hook, chopped worms to attract fish to a worm bait or tiny morsels of cheese fed into a river when fishing cheese to chub.

It is of little use to throw the groundbait into the water unless it goes where the hook bait lies. For this reason many leger fishermen use a swim feeder (fig. 25). When packed with groundbait it is cast out on the line and acts as both an accurate method of laying a trail of attractive bait particles and as a leger weight to enable the hook to hold the bottom.

Some species of coarse fish are attracted by the action of stirring up the mud at the bottom of a lake or pond. Carp and tench are both fish that spend time rooting in the mud for small worms and other invertebrate organisms. If we pull a rake through a swim these fish will tend to investigate the disturbance thinking that other fish have found food and are working the mud. Raking the bottom of a river or stream will also encourage fish to feed because the loosened silt and gravel contains many small creatures that will be washed downstream to waiting mouths.

Places where cattle come to a river to drink are often good holding areas for fish for the animals will stir up mud and disturb water plants as they drink. Downstream about ten or twenty yards is the place to search and cast for your waiting fish.

Artificial baits

Apart from spinning lures and flies, which will be dealt with later in the book, I have little faith in the artificial lures supposedly intended for fishing in freshwater.

Rubber worms, plastic frogs and maggots lack several essential things — taste, smell and of course action or movement which is natural. I have yet to find them better or even comparable to the natural bait and certainly fish can tell the difference!

Fig. 25 *A plastic swimfeeder, provided with a strong nylon link to the swivel. The weight of the feeder can be adjusted by fixing lead strip of different sizes to the body.*

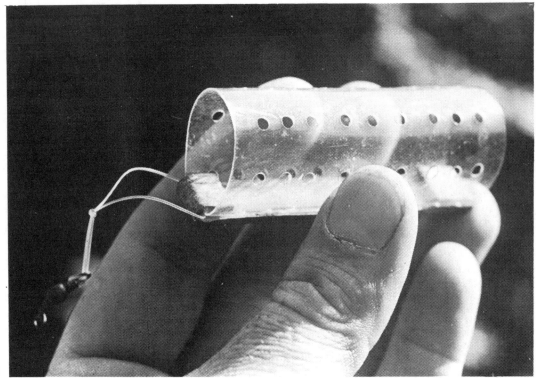

34

How can a large fish be weighed
without harm to the specimen?
Use the landing net and weigh
the fish in it. Then subtract the net
weight from the total. Never hang a fish
on the hook of the spring balance.

Chapter 3
Float fishing methods: rivers and streams

Trotting

A method of fishing in fairly fast water, trotting can be highly productive in that a large area is covered by the bait. Having found a swim that is clear of weed downstream for a distance of thirty yards or so, shot your line so as to present your bait just tripping the bottom. A fairly stout float, capable of supporting the bait and shot and of being seen over distance in the rough water, is essential. Swing cast the end tackle into the water and allow the float to begin trotting downstream. The current speed at the surface may well vary from that at the bottom so some degree of control over the float is necessary. By raising the tip of your rod the float can be checked in its flow which will allow the bait to run down the stream slightly ahead of the float. If the float goes ahead of the hook bait a bite will be hard to detect. As the bed of most rivers is not even and there are natural obstructions to the passage of the bait, the float will often dip below the surface. Only experience will tell you whether the movement was from an obstruction or a fish. When the float has reached the end of the swim it is a good practice to check the peeling of the line from the reel and pause before reeling in. This will have the effect of swinging the bait up toward the surface as in fig. 1. Any fish lurking in

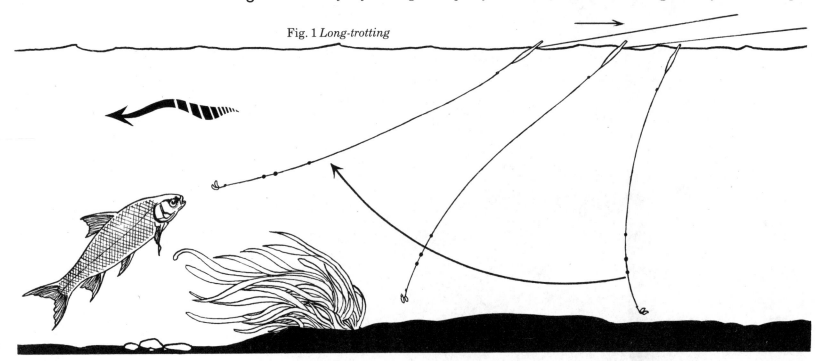

Fig. 1 *Long-trotting*

36

Long-trotting on a Southern chalk-stream. Although primarily a game fish river, there are superb coarse fish to be taken in the slow glides. The angler has to stand in the river because the swim is under the far bank. It is almost impossible to fish from that side due to the overgrown condition of the bank. Roach, dace, chub, barbel and grayling were taken from this stretch.

Deep glide

Shallows

Dace

Roach

Pike

Overhanging
bushes

Deep
undercut
bank

Pike   Chub   Perch

Pike

Dace

Deep hole and back eddy

Shallows

oach

Deep undercut bank

Perch

A small but deep river, generally slow-running but with occasional shallows over which the current flow speeds rapidly. There must be many river situations such as this around the country. This is a purely theoretical analysis of which species might dwell in the river and where.

Because the banks are rather steep and undercut by the winter flood water innumerable lies have been formed for the predators to take up residence. Pike, small because the river is subject to annual flooding and abstraction which tends to keep the shoal fish on the move seeking quiet stretches and constant food supplies. Perch that linger under the banks to harry the fry of each new season. And chub that gather below the bushes to feed on the harvest that rains down from above their heads.

The dace keep to the shallows where there is a constant supply of food washed down from the higher reaches and they are relatively safe from the larger predators. Shoals of roach can be found lying just out of the main current, alongside beds of weed and at the root clumps of the reedmace and bulrushes.

39

It is not always easy to read a river or to fish it! Heavy winter rains (below) on the River Avon remove the shape of the river. One is only able to guess at the location of particular species.
A difficult swim on a small river (right). The stream is twenty feet wide and there is a bank of reeds between the angler and his fish. He played the fish out and, keeping a tight line, drew it through a small gap in the weed thicket. This is a typical perch swim. The fish lie close-in under the roots of the reeds, and, cannot be fished to from the far bank.

weed may be induced to strike at the bait as it rises.

Strong currents and the likelihood of big fish demand strength in the tackle. For long-trotting I use a twelve-feet rod, of Avon action, with plenty of power because the strike has to lift a lot of line before setting the hook! I know that exponents of the art of trotting will say that the centre-pin reel is the right one for this form of fishing but a fixed spool can be used. Open the bale arm and check the line by applying finger pressure as

the line slips over the rim of the bobbin. I like to use fairly strong line (4-5 lbs. B/S) so that I can play most fish back up the stream to my fishing position. Going down stream to a big fish is sometimes essential but often will frighten other fish away.

Swimming the stream

Unlike the previous method, where the angler fishes downstream, swimming the stream is done in an arc around the angler's pitch. The bait is cast upstream and allowed to swim past until finally reaching the downstream extremity of the line, where it is checked, reeled in and recast. Useful on slow-running rivers and streams it is a more delicate method than trotting. But once again the angler must be in constant contact with his float. By lifting the rod-tip as the float comes toward the centre of the swim and lowering the tip as the float passes the angler almost a tight line can be assured.

Tackle should be light, 2-3 lbs. B/S line with a quill float shotted low down on the hook link to keep the bait down in the current. The rod can be lighter in build because the amount of line to be picked up on the strike is not excessive. Hooks size 12-18 depending on the type and size of hook-bait. Try to cast your tackle with the minimum of disturbance because shoal fish, such as roach and dace, will soon leave your swim if disturbed. Small morsels of hook bait thrown in at the head of the swim every few minutes will hold fish in the swim.

A nicely conditioned roach, taken laying-on in the River Bure, Norfolk.

Fig. 2
Laying-on rig

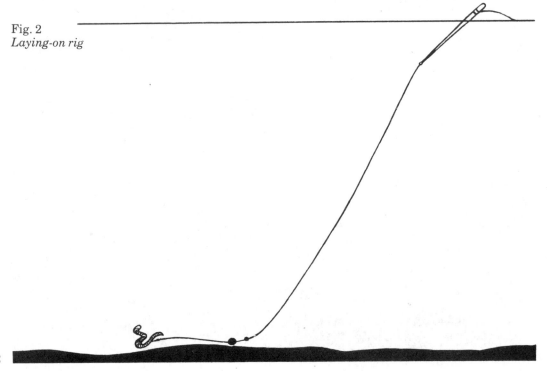

Laying-on

This method is used to fish a bait, in a river current, in a fixed position yet having a float to aid the detection of bites. Make up the rig as shown (fig. 2), a couple of split shots heavy enough to hold bottom against the current flow with a long float just substantial enough to ride the flow and be readily seen. It is worth noting that the float does not have to support the weight of shot or the bait, both lie on the bottom. Keep a fairly tight line to the rig which should be cast down and across the stream, don't tighten to the float immediately but allow the tackle to wash round in the current finding its own natural lie. When the tackle has settled tighten the line and await the bites, which can be of two main types. Either a sliding away under the surface of the float as the fish moves downstream or, if the fish is stationary, the float may lift and lie flat on the water as the fish mouths the bait. Laying-on is at its best in the difficult backwaters, places where you cannot swim a bait down to waiting fish or between rafts of streamer weed where a free-flowing tackle would become hopelessly entangled.

Float paternostering

Again a float fishing method where the bait is fished in a stationary position. But here (fig. 3) the bait is fished at a definite height above the bed of the river. Such obstructions as heavy weed on the bottom, debris or just deep soft mud would prevent a fish from even seeing a bait in

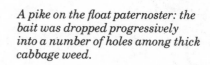

Fig. 3

A pike on the float paternoster: the bait was dropped progressively into a number of holes among thick cabbage weed.

Float paternoster rig for perch or pike angling where the fish are lying in deep holes or where the livebait has to be presented above a blanket of weed.

these conditions. The answer is float paternostering. Most hook baits can be fished in this way but the tackle system is particularly useful when fishing a worm to perch (as in the illustration) or a livebait to river pike. A bomb weight to hold the bottom, a three-way swivel for attachment of the hook link and a cork-bodied float form the rig.

If the water is exceptionally deep the float can be of the sliding variety, running freely on the line and stopped with a stop knot or a short length of bicycle tyre valve rubber clove-hitched onto the line.

Stret-pegging

Stret-pegging differs from trotting or swimming the stream in that both those methods move the bait downstream at the speed of the current. The angler has complete control over the speed at which the bait is fished with the current. Similar in tackle make-up to laying on, the rig has sufficient lead pinched onto the line about three inches from the hook to hold bottom. The water depth is found and a thin but fairly large float is set at about a couple of feet over the depth of water. This measurement can vary, depending on the current strength. The idea is to cast the tackle downstream of the rod-tip and allow the bait to settle. Should no bites occur the rod-tip is raised, a little line is run off the reel which will allow the current to sweep down the lead and bait. If the amount that the rod is raised can be accurately controlled the bait should be dropped downstream in little steps of a foot at a time.

A cold winter's morn on the River Kennet (far left). Not a day for sitting still on the bank, better to work a bait through the deep holes and under the bankside for a chub. These fish have grown well in the stockpond. After inspection and sorting for size they will be transported in oxygenated tanks to improve the fishing in a far-off river.

46

Chapter 4
Float fishing in still water: lakes, ponds and gravel pits

A secluded backwater in a naturalised gravel pit. There is an excellent habitat for fish and other wild life, and peace for the fisherman.

WHEN fishing in rivers, canals and streams the type of bite one gets to a bait often depends not so much on the way in which a fish will take the bait as the conditions in which one is fishing. Fast running water, indeed any water with appreciable current flow will normally give a very definite type of bite. River-dwelling species are conditioned to having food brought to them by the flow of the stream. They see it for a short time as it rolls toward them, make up their minds and take it. Stillwater fish, on the other hand, have time to inspect an offering whether on a hook or otherwise. Presentation of the bait therefore is more important and bait detecting methods have to be more sensitive. Because of this I would first like to deal with three methods of bait presentation which have a high degree of sensitivity built into the rig.

The lift-float

Tench are fish that inhabit still water, they are relatively shy feeders that spend much of their feeding time rooting around in the mud at the bottom of lakes, ponds and canals. Often their presence in a particular water is shown by the continuous streams of bubbles which rise to the surface as they feed. They will often play with a bait without actually taking it and very infuriating that can be. Some years ago Fred. J. Taylor, a very fine fisherman indeed, gave the angling world a method devised to tell the angler exactly when a tench had a bait inside its mouth.

A combination of float and leger fishing, it is called the lift-float method. Attach a light quill or stick float by just the bottom ring to the reel line. Pinch on a swan shot at about 1-1½ inches from the hook. The float should be adjusted for depth so that it lays flat on the surface of the water. The line from the reel is then tightened so that the float cocks under tension (fig. 1). When a fish takes the

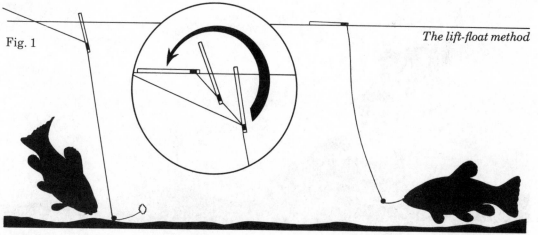

Fig. 1

The lift-float method

Always a tricky moment. Slide the landing net under the fish, at the same time raise the rod tip to draw the fish across the rim of the net. Perform the operation positively but unhurriedly and the fish is yours!

bait into its mouth it lifts the shot from the bottom and the float having no weight to carry rises in the water and falls flat on the surface. I tend to strike when the float is in the act of falling flat, as I have found that to wait until it lies flat often means that the fish has taken the bait and is in the process of ejecting the hook. The lift-float method will also take other species — big bream tend to feed in the same way as tench, due, no doubt, to the fact that their body shape forces them to stand on their heads to take a morsel from the bottom. Shy-biting carp can also be fished for in this way.

Over-shotting the float

Sometimes roach and other small bottom feeding species will give almost undetectable bites. The float hardly bobs and I find it extremely difficult to decide whether to strike or allow the bite to develop into a more positive pull. One way in which the sensitivity of light float tackle can be improved is to over-shot the rig. To tackle up choose a float capable of carrying a definite amount of weight, say, three number 1 shot. Pinch four shot onto the line and adjust the float to allow the bait and one of the shot to lie on the bottom. When a fish takes the bait a bite is registered by the float sliding away under the surface. The reason is that where formerly three shot were suspended and supported by the float, four now weight the line. The bite is therefore indicated by the leads pulling the float down rather than the fish (fig. 2).

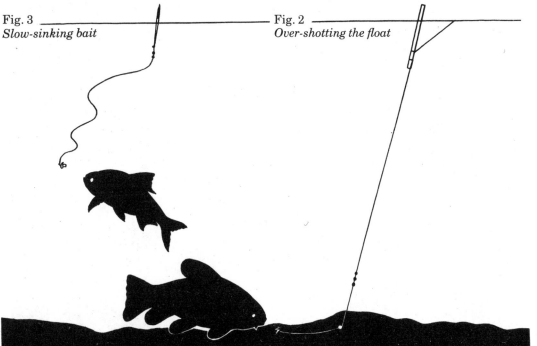

Fig. 3 _____
Slow-sinking bait

Fig. 2 _____
Over-shotting the float

Slow-sinking baits

Quite often fish, particularly rudd, will be found feeding on minute organisms just below the surface of the water. If a handful of maggots are thrown in the rudd will dash to and fro feeding vigorously but they will ignore the maggot hook bait fished just below the float. I think the reason is that the hooked maggot lacks that natural wiggle and twirl that a free-falling grub would exhibit as it sinks to the depths. Now if the rig is made in such a way that the float is cocked by the correct number of shot placed immediately below the float, but allowing a couple of feet of nylon unimpeded by weight, the maggot bait will fall through the water more naturally. Bites appear to increase in number using this method. Keep a constant dribble of maggots going into the swim to both draw and hold fish in the area (fig. 3).

Two of the running-water rigs can be used in still water, as both laying-on and float paternostering are suitable methods for taking bottom feeding and mid-water swimming species.

The illustration (fig. 4) shows how strong wind can cause a belly in the line between the rod tip and the float. This belly will take away a great deal of the sensitivity of your rig, more so if the float is fixed to the line by the bottom ring and cap at the top. If the float, which should be an antennae, is fixed by a single rubber at its base and the rod tip is sunk under the surface of the water and line reeled in to cock the float, wind will have

Father and son fish in the warm autumn sunshine.

49

little effect upon the behaviour of the float. The antennae stick presents little surface to the wind and bites will be detected either as a sinking away or by the float rising and falling flat on the water.

There has been a considerable argument in the fishing world about the relative methods of fishing for pike. Being the largest and greediest predator in freshwater, this fish will take live and dead fish of most species. Traditionally livebaits, either roach or rudd, were used as hook baits for the pike. In the past twenty years deadbaiting has become more and more popular. I will not argue the ethics of using livebaits here, sufficient to say that each angler must make up his own mind as to whether he wants to fish the method. I would say that deadbait angling seems to take fewer fish but they seem to be the larger specimens.

To fish a livebait one can use the hook rig known as a snap tackle (Chapter 2, fig. 11), similar to the herring rig. The end treble hook would be fixed into the livebait by one point just behind the gill case and the second treble attached just behind the dorsal fin, slightly higher than in the herring rig. A small Jardine spiral lead (Chapter 6, fig. 3) can be attached to the line to keep the livebait down in the water, fix it at a point midway between the swivel and the float. Most of the floats used in the past for pike fishing were heavy bulbous affairs, easily seen by the fisherman but presenting a massive resistance to the fish when it tried to move off with the bait.

Fishing an Essex gravel pit for rudd.

Quite often the bait was mouthed, then dropped by the pike, which resulted in the livebait being killed for no reason.

Use a pike float of slim shape just capable of supporting the livebait, and lead if you choose to use one. Try to resist the urge to cast the livebait out onto the water, the impact will either kill it or stun it thereby defeating the whole object of using an attractive live fish to lure the predator. A lively bait will generally swim off drawing the float along behind it. A pike run, as we call the bite, is often preceded by a violent jigging of the float as the livebait tries to escape the attentions of a pike. If the pike takes the bait he will move off with the float either diving below the surface or perhaps skating across it. Let the run go, then when the fish stops put the reel into gear and strike as the second run starts. This should ensure that the pike is hooked in the mouth and not in the throat.

Small livebaits, such as dace or minnows can be fished on a single-hook rig tied to a short length of wire trace. The wire is very important because the teeth of a pike are extremely sharp and can easily bite through strong nylon. A reel line of about 8-12 lbs. B/S on a light multiplier or fixed-spool reel and a rod capable of handling a big fish make up the pike-fisher's gear.

Floating bait

No float is used for this form of angling. Crust is normally the bait and carp the quarry. The crust is used as hook bait, the hook tied direct to the reel line. Sufficient weight for casting is gained by dipping the crust momentarily in the water so that it absorbs just a little. Don't make it soggy or you will find the crust flying off the hook during the cast. Carp have a habit, at certain times during the season, of patrolling the reeded margins of a lake cleaning up any food that they find floating on the surface. It is good fishing to toss a few crusts along the lake edges and place a hook bait among them, then with the bale arm of the reel open wait for a carp to pick up your hook-bait. Let the fish run and when you are sure that it has the bait close the bale arm and strike positively to pull the hook from the crust.

Occasionally the floating crusts will attract rudd, smaller pieces and lighter end tackle will give lively sport with these golden-flanked beauties.

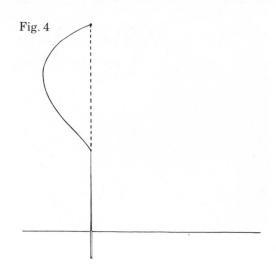

Fig. 4

A Shropshire mere — extremely good coarse fishing can be found in the huge expanse of this type of water. Bream are the quarry, though other species are present.

Chapter 5
Legering

LEGERING, whether practised in still or running water, is a most versatile form of angling. The tackle and methods used can be readily adapted for almost any fishing situation. The system depends on using a weight to present a bait on the bottom, either stationary or as a rolling bait, to fish to definite areas of the river or lake bed. The illustration (fig. 1) shows three ways in which the leger weight can be attached. Probably the simplest form of running leger is an Arlesey Bomb (1), which has a swivel set into the lead at its head and is run onto the main line. The lead is stopped by a pinched-on split lead giving the required amount of trail for the hook link which has the hook tied direct to the line. The amount of trail, distance between hook and lead, depends largely on current flow strength and whether the hook bait is needed to wash around at a distance from its tethering lead.

A variable shot link-leger, suggested by Fred J. Taylor (2). It is most useful when the weight needed to hold bottom varies throughout a swim and is formed by folding a short length of strong nylon over the reel line to which is added a number of pinched on swan shot. Not only can the weight of leads be finely adjusted but in the event that the lead becomes entangled in the bottom a sharp pull will strip the leads from the link freeing the

A slow-moving river (right), *the Medway at Teston. Deep and snag-free, it provides good sport for the coarse fisherman. In winter the higher reaches of the Great Ouse* (centre) *fish well for chub, found among the tangles of dying reeds and beneath over-hanging trees. Keep the rod tip up or apply side strain to a powerful fighter* (far right). *Never point the rod at the fish, the strain is then all on the knots and line. Natural spring in the rod blank is a cushion against sudden movement from the hooked fish causing a line breakage.*

hook. Should you have a fish which dives into weed or some other underwater obstruction the lead often becomes fouled and prevents you from working the fish out of the weed. In a situation like this the link-leger helps to free the end tackle.

Fred Buller's swimfeeder-leger (3), is used to provide an accurately placed supply of groundbait, in the chosen swim, as close as possible to the hook. Although intended for fishing in running water, the technique has applications in still-water fishing. Let us first consider the use of a swim feeder. To throw out ones groundbait in such a way as to place it accurately every time in the position that you want to fish, is difficult. I find that by

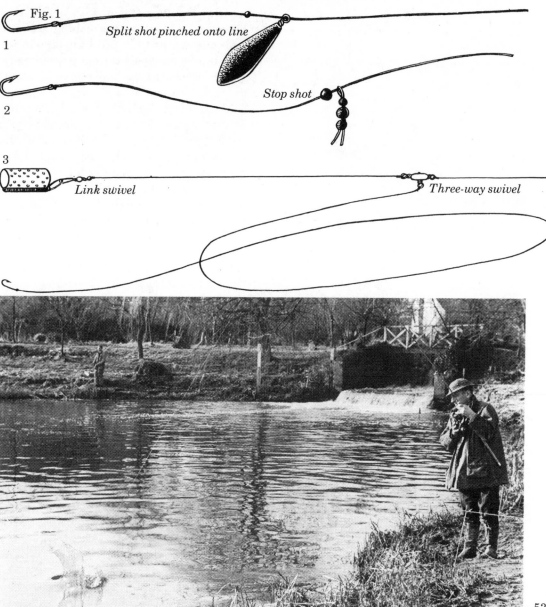

Fig. 1

1   *Split shot pinched onto line*

2   *Stop shot*

3   *Link swivel*   *Three-way swivel*

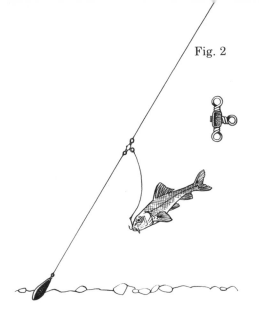

Fig. 2

loading the swimfeeder with particles of hookbait, casting to the fishing position and giving a lusty heave I am able to lay a trail of groundbait far more accurately. Having repeated the move several times one can be assured that there is enough feed to attract fish to the hook. In running water fishing, the next cast would be to a point just slightly downstream of the groundbaited area. The hook would have been baited, the swimfeeder filled and allowed to swim around in the current and settle naturally. The groundbait would then spill gradually from the feeder, dribbling past the hookbait. Fish downstream of the hook would notice the arrival of food, start feeding and then move up to meet the free-flowing morsels inevitably arriving at the baited hook.

A simpler form of positioning groundbait is to attach it to the leger weight by pressing it firmly around the lead but it may fly off during the cast.

In still-water the technique has to be slightly different. There is no current to wash the groundbait out of the feeder so one must cast the swimfeeder and release the food by striking it out of the tube. Maggot fishing allows one a slightly different system, load the swimfeeder with maggots but seal both ends of the tube with flake. The grubs will then wriggle from the tube via the holes bored in its sides. Ensure though that these holes are big enough for maggots to escape.

There is another form of bottom fishing with which to present a livebait to

Fig. 3 *Make certain that the line runs freely through the rod rings and is not trapped between the rod and rest. Different strengths of current can be fished with sensitivity by varying the weight of the dough bobbin.*

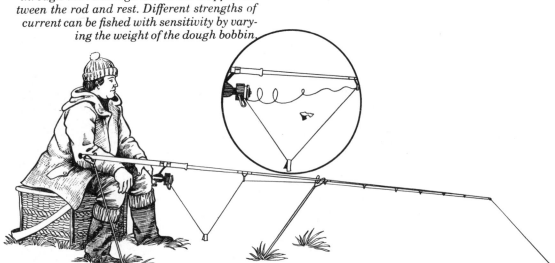

The author with a first fish of the season! A mirror carp from a farm pool in Suffolk.

perch or other predators and it is called the leger-paternoster (fig. 2). Quite simply it involves fishing a hook-link at a pre-determined distance from the leger weight attached to a three-way swivel. This rig can be presented as a stationary tackle or, by raising the rod tip and giving a little line, can be made to trot the bait downstream to search out fish lies.

Bite detection

There are a multitude of ways in which a bite can be detected using leger methods. Possibly the simplest is just to rely on a knock or tremble of the rod tip. Unfortunately, this method allows a fish to feel the tension on the line although in a hard-running stream this may make little difference to a hungry fish. More sophisticated ways to detect bites have been arrived at, over the past decade. The dough bobbin is the cheapest and is similar in use to the folded silver paper indicator (fig. 3). After the cast has been made, slack line is wound in and a piece of bread dough or a folded slip of silver paper is hung on the line between the reel and the first rod ring. A bite from a taking fish will show as the indicator jumps up from its hanging position. This method allows for the fish to move off with the bait without feeling the line tension. A dough bobbin can, of course, be hung from the line leaving the tip ring but this will involve getting up from your stool to fix the indicator every time you make a cast.

In recent years the swing-tip and

The villain of the water—a pike that was brought to the net after it took a rudd that was being played on light tackle. Although not hooked in any way, the pike refused to let go of its meal.

quiver tip have appeared. Both of these items of tackle are screwed into the threaded tip ring (that all good leger rods should have) and indicate a bite by the raising of the flexible extension to the rod tip. They are extremely sensitive indicators and most of them allow a degree of adjustment to the length of the swinging section. Fast biting fish would necessitate a short swinging action, whilst wary biters require a longer time to take a bait and so one should give the indicator a longer length and so greater time for a bite to develop (fig. 4).

The position of the angler's body and the lie of the rod in its rests, relative to the line angle, are very important. The leger rod lying in two rests at right angles to the bankside is shown in the illustration (fig. 5). A strike backwards, at right angles to the line, should pick up the line and give direct penetration to the hook. With the rod tip pointed toward the line one can only strike up and over the right shoulder. This means that the rod has to be swung through a considerable arc before the line begins to move at the lead and a hookhold effected. Position the rests and the fishing chair or stool so that the hand hovers over the butt of the rod ready for an instant reaction to indicator movement.

A third bite indicator, and incidentally one that you can make for yourself, is the spring-bite indicator (fig. 6). It is made by bending a length of 16 S.W.G. spring steel wire to the shape shown. This is fixed to a bankstick about three feet

Golden beauties — rudd from a lake in East Anglia.

long and bound on with adhesive tape. The indicator is positioned beyond the front rod rest and arranged so that the smaller of the curves in the wire is a foot ahead of the rod tip and on the same level.

Once again the rod rests are set up to allow fishing at right angles to the line direction. After casting the bait out and allowing the lead to settle, the line is hooked over the bite detector and the rod set down on the rests. The line is then wound in to put the spring under tension. Two types of bite can easily be seen: if the spring pulls down a fish has picked up the bait and is moving away from the angler; if the fish moves toward the rod a slack line bite will be shown by the spring lifting up to an untensioned position. To aid reaction to movement of the indicator slip a length of bicycle tyre valve rubber around the small bend in the wire and paint the rubber in bright, contrasting colours.

Night fishing, particularly for carp, has brought about the production of electric bite indicators. These operate on the basis that the line is hooked over a lever which is spring loaded. The bale arm of the reel is left open with the line free to run-off from the spool but in so doing it creates a tension against the indicator lever which closes contacts and sets off a buzzer.

A cheaper and simpler form of bite detector, for night fishing, is the silver paper slip mentioned earlier. Again the bale arm is open and the line is made to lie on a sheet of newspaper or similar

Fig. 4

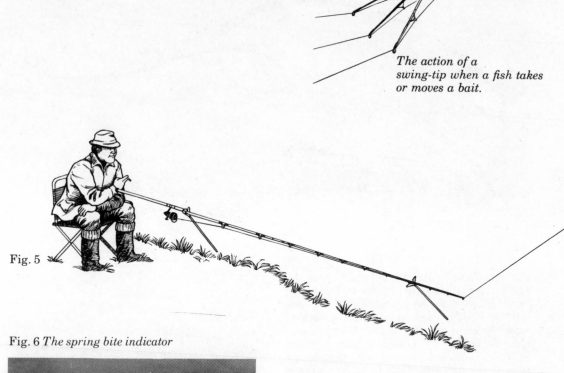

The action of a swing-tip when a fish takes or moves a bait.

Fig. 5

Fig. 6 *The spring bite indicator*

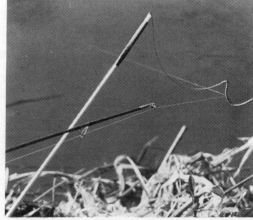

57

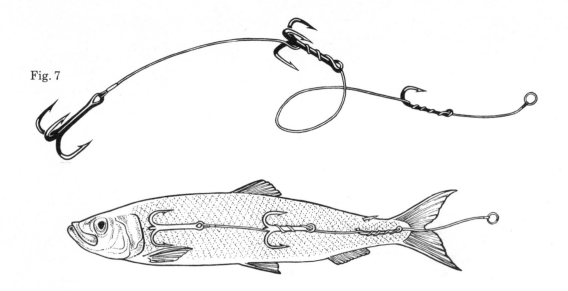

Fig. 7

The end treble is attached by one hook to the bait at a point behind the gill-case. The bait is then hooked onto the second treble half-way along the body and a single hook is used to make the trace firm to the tail. This prevents casting the bait off although tying the bait on with elasticated thread makes the herring more secure and less likely to be torn off by a pike. The single hook and thread would be positioned just in front of the tail.

Thick weed in this river (right) forces the angler to lift his fish hard. Any delay in getting the fish on the move would allow it to dive into the roots. Fine fish from a swim in the Royalty Fishery on the Hampshire Avon (centre). A barbel and six chub taken legering among the weeded patches. After netting and perhaps photographing your fish return it to the water as quickly as possible (far right). Support the fish in an upright position and let it swim off in its own time.

material. A slip of silver paper is folded over the line and if a fish picks up the bait and moves away the paper will rustle as it is dragged forward. In daylight hours the same indicators can usefully be employed, carp fishing is sometimes slow and the use of an audible warning device allows the angler to give his attention to other things!

Pike fishing with a deadbait is a form of legering where no lead is used. The weight of a herring or sprat provides sufficient weight for casting. The bait is mounted on a pre-formed wire trace (fig. 7) connected via a swivel direct to the reel line and cast out. The rod can be placed in its rests with the bale arm open and an indicator used to show the begin-

ning of a take. As the strike has to be delayed, to give the pike time to take the bait into its mouth, an indicator is not really necessary but we all like to see something happening!

A word about lines and hooks. It is difficult to suggest line strengths for every fishing situation, but generally one should ally the breaking strain to three things, the speed and pull of the current, weight of bait to be cast and the size of the fish expected. Hook size is determined by the size of the bait in use and by the type and size of fish.

Seek advice from anglers who are already having success on the water, it is rare to find a man who is not willing to assist.

Chapter 6
Spinning in freshwater

HERE is a fishing technique often referred to as 'chuck it and chance it' fishing. That statement could not be further from the truth for spinning, and by that I mean all the ways that one can spin, troll or flutter a bait, is a fine art. It is not for the lazy angler who likes to settle himself into a chair and remain immobile for the rest of the day, nor is it for the man who does not bother to learn how to read a water.

Spinning properly depends on a number of mechanical actions. Most important is the angler's ability to cast not only distance, but with accuracy. The basic pattern (as shown on the left) is the overhead cast. A sight (fig. 1) is taken by pointing the rod at the point to which the bait is going to be cast, then with the bale arm open the rod is swung back over the shoulder. With a quick flick the rod is returned to its former position and during this movement the bait is released, just as the wrist passes the eye. Spinning with a double-handed rod is slightly different. The rod cannot be taken over the shoulder in a perfectly upright fashion, it is more at an angle across the body (fig. 2). I have depicted a fixed-spool reel, but a multiplier can be used.

The type of rod rather depends on the size of bait, type of fish and distance needed to be covered with the cast. Generally, light baits and small fish can best be handled on the single-handed rod. Big rivers and big fish require larger baits, stronger tackle and a longer rod to provide the leverage necessary to land the fish. Sometimes there is insufficient weight in the lure so we attach a spinning lead (fig. 3). 1 is a wye lead incorporating a swivel. It serves also as a means of preventing the line from twisting due to the revolving motion of some spinning baits. 2 is a simple fold-over lead, pressed over the line it will also stop line twist but needs to be used in conjunction with a swivel. 3 is another form, the Hardy anti-kink lead. 4. The Jardine spiral lead is a

Fig. 1

Fig. 2

weight that can be bent at its middle to act as a keel and to smooth out line twist when used with a swivel. It does, but unfortunately tends to unravel itself from the line. The trace shown is a wire one. For pike spinning, about twenty pounds B/S is necessary, having a swivel for connecting the reel line and a link-swivel to attach the lure. A similar set-up in nylon will serve when angling for perch, trout or salmon. The zander, however, has sharp teeth like the pike and needs to be fished with a wire trace.

There must be hundreds of artificial baits and all probably catch fish at sometime or another. A variety of pike baits, shown in fig. 4, may be needed to cover all your water on a spinning day. Let us consider their construction and uses. (a) is a wobbler, a silver bar that flashes through the water with an erratic motion and simulates the action of a wounded fish. (b) is a spinning lure, the Devon minnow, most often used for trout and salmon but good for pike. The body is formed as a tube with two fins that cause it to revolve on a wire flight (fig. 5). Made of wood or metal, it will then fish just under the surface or at depth. The bead prevents the body sliding down onto the treble hook. For fishing in very deep water the wire flight can have a small amount of lead wire wrapped around it to give the bait more weight. These minnows come in different lengths and colours. (c) is a jointed plug and has an irregular swimming action. Available as a floater or sinker you can cover water in depth

Fig. 3

An unusual plug with a deep-diving, erratic action very attractive to pike.

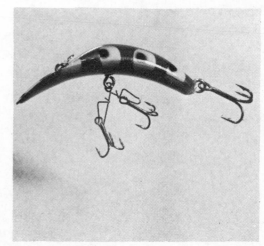

Fig. 4 *A selection of artificial spinning baits.*   Fig. 5 *Devon minnow body and wire flight.*

with this plug. The diving vane can also be adjusted to alter the plug's action. (d) is an old favourite of mine, the Colorado spoon. Made of metal, it has enough body weight to cast well and is painted red on the interior of the spoon section so that on retrieve it flashes red and silver alternately. This bait spins well when being only slowly wound in, a useful action when you want to let a fish get a good look at the lure. (e) The weedless spoon intended for spinning over or through, as the manufacturers say, thick weed. The hook is engaged in the body of the bait and only emerges when a fish takes it into its mouth. (f) is a first class spinning lure, as is (g). The spoon revolves around a bar on a saddle. It flashes, according to colour and vibrates on the retrieve. Fig. 6 shows the bait in detail. Various sizes and weights can be had but even the smallest casts well.

The plug (h) can be made to wobble or swerve and dive to any depth, depending on the method of retrieve. Made in wood or plastic it is a killing lure. Lure (i) is another wobbling spoon, similar to (a), but having a greater bend like a 'lazy S' along its length. This imparts a violent swerving motion to the fish-shaped spoon.

The floating bait (fig. 7) is good for spinning over weed beds where plants come almost to the surface. It flashes and wobbles attracting pike out of the haven of weed by the action which simulates that of a wounded or frightened small fish.

Spinning on stillwater

Pike like to lie up in holts, an under-cut bank, the depths of a hole and often among the roots of a fallen tree. From their vantage point they can watch and wait, for their colouring makes an ideal camouflage. A pike's body is built for speed, the way in which he runs after grabbing a bait is something to watch and his run is so often back into the hiding place. Select a position where you can cover the water, fan-casting your lure, but also giving yourself room in which to play the fish out into the open water.

Give him a slack line or let him get back to an obstruction and he will probably break your line or shed the hooks. Fan casting is a useful plan of action when spinning, it covers all of the available fishing area thoroughly. If there is a lazy fish within range (one that does not come to the spun bait but is interested) he will see the bait, possibly move toward it and turn away. The next cast, although on a slightly different line may well hook the fish. Always fish the cast out, right to the bank. Keep the lure working until it reaches your feet, for a pike or perch will often follow the lure and take it as you are preparing to lift the bait for the next cast. You must use a short wire trace when spinning for pike, it can be bought ready made or made up from a piece of Elasticum wire with a swivel to connect the reel line and a snap link for attaching lures.

Perch and trout are fished for with the

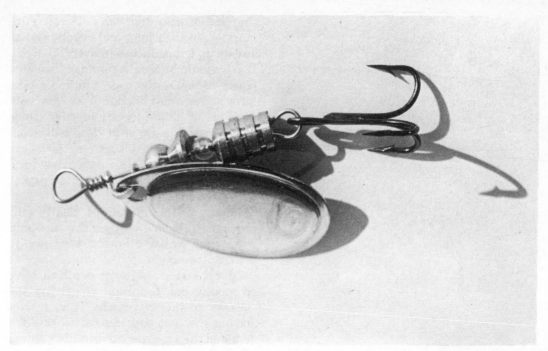

Fig. 6 *Weighted spoon with revolving blade.*

Fig. 7 *A floating plug fished across weedbeds.*

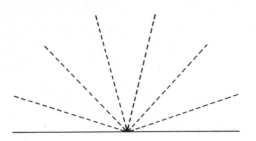

smallest of spinning baits. Devon minnows of an inch long and revolving bar spoons up to two inches in overall length. Perch should be sought in much the same places as you would expect to find a pike lying. They also strike from ambush, are fond of hiding in or alongside dense beds of weed. A lot of anglers will avoid casting into such places as they fear losing what can be an expensive lure. If we want to catch fish we must expect to lose the odd bait!

Most of the situations dealt with previously involve casting the lure and retrieving whilst allowing the lure to provide the action.

For covering a water in depth we have to modify our technique by giving the bait yet another movement. This involves letting the bait sink almost to the bottom and then recovering it in little spurts of winding and pausing. The action of the lure is to move forward and up in the water, then to stop and flutter downwards before again moving forwards. The system is called *sink-and-draw* and will take fish that are lying on the bottom or cruising in midwater. It is a killing method and one that ensures that all areas across the length, breadth and depth of your fan casting have seen the bait. All heavy baits, plugs, wobblers and spinners are suitable for sink-and-draw fishing.

Spinning on rivers and streams

Very similar spinning methods to those used on stillwater can be applied on river. On slow-running streams, fan casting will prove its value. On the faster river progressive movement by the angler, taking a pace down the bank after each cast, is the order. Cast across the water and allow the current to swing the bait round in an arc. The depth at which the bait fishes will depend on the weight of bait, speed of current and the use of a spinning lead on the line. As the bait reaches a point under the bank, downstream of you, begin to slowly turn the reel handle to recover the line. Fish may have seen and followed the bait on its journey and are often encouraged to strike as the bait moves slowly upstream. Again fish each cast out to your feet.

If you experience a pull to the bait, a half-hearted take by the fish which does not hook it cast again and return the bait over the lie. If there is no repeat offer change the bait for one of another colour or size. If once more you are unsuccessful leave the fish for a time and return to the same casting position later in the day.

Spinning with a natural bait

Most artificial baits rely on their action to take fish—very few look at all like a natural fish or animal. They succeed because they simulate the swimming activity of a living creature. A natural appearance can sometimes be important

Fig. 8

Far left: *Good fishing for a soft winter's day. A posie of average-size river pike taken on plugs and spinning lures.* Centre: *A salmon breaks water; it was hooked by Brian Harris fishing the River Lune at Kirkby Lonsdale.*

particularly when pike fishing. Because of this anglers often spin a dead fish. I prefer the wobbling tackle (fig. 8) easily made up by the angler from wire, three trebles and a single hook. The idea is to attach the hooks in such a way as to impart a twist to the body of the dead fish. On retrieve the spun bait will perform wide spiralling movements very attractive to the predatory pike. The extent to which the bait will gyrate depends on the positioning of the treble hook and the amount of bend formed in the body of the bait. For large pike, such as are found in deep lakes, herring is probably better than small roach or rudd. Being relatively soft, one may have to tie the herring onto the trace with elasticated thread which can be bought from any haberdashery.

Take a pair of forceps and a pike gag with you when you fish for this species. Multiple-hook lures can be difficult to remove and the gag will enable you to clear the hooks without tearing your hands to pieces on the incredibly sharp teeth of this fish. It's advisable to file down the crude points found on most gags, as they can sink into the jaw of the fish and cause considerable injury.

Spinning can be undertaken from a boat. On waters such as the Norfolk Broads, the Irish lakes and other vast stretches of water many of the pikey places are unfishable from the bank. Casting to the reed margins and other fish lies is profitable but only if you can get the fish away from the natural obstructions. To fish into the banks from a boat enables the angler to draw the hooked fish out into clear water where it can be played out in safety.

Land the fish with a landing net of adequate proportions and after unhooking return it to the water—don't attempt to put pike into a keepnet!

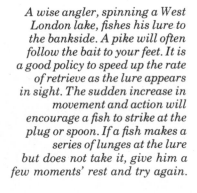

A wise angler, spinning a West London lake, fishes his lure to the bankside. A pike will often follow the bait to your feet. It is a good policy to speed up the rate of retrieve as the lure appears in sight. The sudden increase in movement and action will encourage a fish to strike at the plug or spoon. If a fish makes a series of lunges at the lure but does not take it, give him a few moments' rest and try again.

The landing net must be large enough to contain the pike. River Stour, Suffolk.

Chapter 7
By the waterside

TO be an angler is to be concerned with nature. Fish and the creatures that they depend upon for their food are part of an eco-system or chain of interdependence. Each animal needs the presence of others, both its own species and entirely different life forms. Let us consider some of the better-known creatures that could be called anglers' companions.

Surely every one of us has taken a stroll by a river or stream and seen a delightfully coloured bird with a vivid red beak and constantly bobbing black and white tail. The moorhen, unmistakable among the native British birds. Although it does not resemble its near relative, the coot, it does unfortunately share many of the bad habits associated with its cousin—a noisy, quarrelsome nature coupled with a taste for the eggs and chicks of other birds.

The moorhen nests close to the waterside, usually in thick cover which gives security, and rarely builds a floating nest. The bird seldom moves far from its own particular stretch of water. Indeed the chicks which result from the several broods reared between March and the middle of summer often take up their own territories close to the scene of their birth. From six to ten eggs are laid in each successive brood and both adult birds share the incubation and rearing of the young. Feeding of the chicks by the brothers and sisters of an earlier brood has also been observed. The diet of these busy little water hens is tremendously varied: invertebrate life, seeds, fruit, and

Moorhen Gallinula chloopus

Brown rat Rattus norvegicus

Robin Erithacus rubecula

naturally most anglers' baits!

As with the coot, the feet are large and unwebbed between the toes. Using a rapid wing-beat and a running ballet-like action of their legs, moorhen seem at times almost to walk on the water.

Let us stroll farther along the bankside to see if that chap has caught anything. He seems preoccupied with something in the scrub behind him. Could be a small vole? No, it is a brown rat, an animal that is so often linked with man. The rat is never far from man or his habitat. Omnivorous in diet, the rat will creep out on to the bank alongside a fisherman, overcoming its natural shyness, to steal whatever crumbs have been dropped.

The brown rat has spread throughout this country, ousting the black rat from most of its former dwelling places. It should never be touched, dead or alive, because it may be carrying diseases that are communicable to human beings.

Did you see that bird fly off into the bushes? Yes, it is a robin. Of all the cheeky blighters one meets on the river bank, this bird must take first place. He was probably stealing from the angler's bait tin. If you take compassion and throw the bird a few maggots, in no time at all he is in the bait tin helping himself! In winter birds become increasingly tame. As the cold weather arrives, bringing heavy frosts that harden the ground, the robin and other members of the thrush family find food harder to come by. The awareness of man's presence dimin-

ishes as hunger begins to control the actions of the birds.

This type of river, a meandering stream, that rises in the chalk country of Salisbury Plain, is rich in weedlife. Huge streamer-like clumps of *Ranunculus* separate the river into a number of narrow channels. The weed is a home for many creatures and these animals provide food for the many large trout that inhabit the river. A prolific weed growth brings the swan, but which of the swans is it? The head has a proud bearing with a black knob at the base of a red bill. It is mute swan. This bird can hardly be called wild; it was introduced into Britain from the Continent and the swans that we see today are descendants from domesticated stock. There are two other species of swan, the whooper and Bewick's, which visit us in the winter. They can be readily identified from the mute swan by their bills which have a colour pattern the direct opposite of the mute swan. They have black bills with yellow patches at the rear of the bill extending to the eyes.

Can you hear that noise coming from the other side of the bridge? Feeding time for the ducks, I should think. Round about this time of the day a couple of old ladies come down from the village to feed the ducks. Summer or winter, they never fail. The ducks know when it is time to expect the handout and grow quite noisy if the food comes late!

Mallard they are, though there are a few hybrids amongst them. See that white

Mute swan Cygnus olor

Whooper swan Cygnus cygnus

Mallard Anas platyrhynchos

Mallard X Aylesbury (hybrid)

Frog Rana temporaria

by permission of UFAW

by permission of UFAW

Toad Bufo bufo

Otter Lutra lutra

duck? That's a cross between a wild mallard and a lumbering Aylesbury from a farmyard flock. Saw them chasing a frog the other day; that is a pretty rare sight these days, I can tell you. When I was a lad there were frogs in every pond. We used to gather the spawn each spring to take to school. That was about the only biology lesson we ever saw. The frog's function in life was to keep down the insect population, but the haphazard use of pesticides has done the frog no good. That, coupled with the filling-in of all the little ponds and roadside ditches, could account for their rarity. I'm not at all sure that the toad isn't extinct in my part of the world. We had one in the garden a few years back, living in the cold-frame among the flowerpots and cucumbers. Do you know the difference between them?

The frog has a blunt head and its skin is usually smooth, brown or yellow in colour. The underparts are spotted and there is sometimes a variation in colour and pattern between males and females. The body of a frog is angular in shape, with long limbs suited to jumping. Those of the toad are short because this creature is slow-moving and crawls on much shorter limbs. The toad is a bulky creature, reddish-brown in colour, with warty growths covering the skin on the back of the amphibian. During the breeding season male toads have black nuptial pads on the inside of the first three fingers of the forelimbs.

Both frogs and toads seek water in

which to breed but most of their lives is spent on land. Frogs will hibernate in water, whereas toads seek a dry spot among rocks or even within barns and garden sheds.

Talking of rarities in the countryside, one animal has truly been decimated, hunted out from the rivers of the South. It's the otter, an animal that takes fish as do human beings. I think that the real reason it has been so persecuted on salmon rivers is because it is a much better fisherman than we are! The diet of the otter is not confined to fish and it will eat practically anything that presents itself —small animals, frogs, insects and in fact a whole host of small creatures. The dog otter does not live with his family but watches over their nightly wanderings from a distance. Sometimes emitting a low-pitched whistle, he lets the bitch and her pups know that he is about.

Come this way on a dark spring night and you may hear an old dog otter that is reputed to use a number of fallen trees for his holts. Under the roots that have been exposed he will dig a resting place. Sometimes, in the early dawn, I've seen an otter close by the reeded banks beyond that copse there. Just a fleeting glimpse as the animal climbed up from the river, its coat glistening with droplets, to shake itself like a retriever and lope off into the wood.

It is not all a tale of disappearing animals in the countryside; now and then a new animal or bird makes an entry into our ecology. Some, like the coypu and mink, are brought by man and not always to the benefit of the other animals. That bird in the tree is a relative newcomer to Britain. It is a collared dove. Back in 1952 this delightful little dove arrived in East Anglia. Within three years it had become a nesting species and now it is spread throughout the land. The bird is instantly recognisable by the black and white collar on its neck. When flying it exhibits a white tip to the tail feathers.

There is a small lake a mile or two down the lane which is home to another introduced bird, a Canada goose. Looking something like the barnacle geese that visit our shores in the winter, it would nest near to the lake if it had a mate. No doubt it lost contact with a flock of these geese and now spends most days grazing in the water-meadows, with an occasional visit to the river.

The goose makes pleasant company when we fish for the carp in the early morning. It goes about its business quietly, unlike the coots that come crashing through the reeds. You can be sitting at your rod, lost in thought, when suddenly the reeds crack apart. With a furious fluttering of wings and splattering of feet a coot will explode into the stillness of the pool.

They are aggressive birds, particularly during the mating season. This starts with building a floating nest tied into the reedmace. A large proportion of any day appears to be spent disputing the boundaries of their territory with neighbours.

Coypu Myocaster coypus

Collared dove Streptopelia decaocto

Canada goose Branta canadensis

Coot Fulica atra

Several broods are hatched each season; six or seven buff eggs with black blotches are laid and incubated by both parents. The coots lose many of their young ones, and pike account for most of them. There is a fox, though, that pays the waterside a regular visit. It isn't often seen, but the marks from the pads are sometimes visible in the soft mud at the water's edge.

These are just a few of the creatures that are regularly seen and that pay the rivers and lakes a visit. Most of them, like us, are anglers, although I often think that they are more accomplished fishers than we are. In your time at the water, when the float sits motionless upon the surface, take a glance around. You may well catch a glimpse of these and other anglers' companions.

Fox Vulpes vulpes

Chapter 8
Rods and reels

Winfield tackle for Freshwater

1. Winfield 'Float Fisher'. An all-action float rod 12 feet long in three pieces, with spigot ferrules. Internally threaded tip ring (for swingtip) and stand-off intermediate rings. Hollow glass fibre construction and light weight make this a fine rod for general coarse fishing.

2. Winfield 'Leger Fisher'. The big fish rod for the man that legers for tench, barbel, carp and chub. 10 ft 6 inches in length, hollow glass fibre in three pieces with threaded tip ring for swing-tip and quiver-tip fishing.

3. Winfield 'Game Spinner'. A 10 ft two-piece rod in hollow glass fibre with a fast tip action for casting large or small baits but capable of handling very big fish. This rod has a locking winch fitting that will accept fixed spool or multiplying reels. Suitable for pike, salmon, pollack and bass spinning.

4. Winfield 'Trout Spinner'. A light two-section rod in hollow glass fibre for spinning. Fast tapered action over the 8 feet length will allow effortless casting for trout, perch and small pike.

5. Winfield 'Fly Caster'. A general-purpose trout fly rod of 8 feet 6 inches, in two pieces with a spigot ferrule. Made in hollow glass fibre, this rod is ultra-light in weight and will cast an AFTM No. 6 line.

6. Winfield 'Coarse Fisher'. A ball-bearing reel of quality. Small in size, weighing 8 ounces. Capacity 170 yards of 6 lbs. nylon. Gear ratio 1-4.1.

7. Winfield 'Spin Fisher'. Larger in capacity. 130 yards of 10 lbs. nylon. The shaft runs on a ball-race. Weight 10 ounces. Gear ratio 1-3.4.

8. Winfield 'Trout Fly'. A centre-pin fly reel that has a large capacity. 150 yards of 15 lbs. backing and an AFTM No. 6 double taper fly line.

9. Winfield 'Spin Caster'. A closed-face fixed-spool reel for the spin fisherman. The capacity is 120 yards of 5 lbs. nylon. Weight 10 ounces. Gear ratio 1-2.3. ▶

Winfield tackle for Saltwater

1. Winfield 'Shore Caster'. An 11 feet beachcaster for cod, bass and general shore fishing. Built in hollow glass, two pieces, with a fast taper action for casting 3-6 ounce leads. Has a locking winch fitting, fully corked handle and breaker ring.

2. Winfield 'Surf Caster'. A hollow glass, two-piece bass rod with spigot ferrule. 10 feet with fully-corked handle and locking winch fitting. Has a large breaker ring for both fixed-spool and multiplying reels. Casts 2-4 ounce leads.

3. Winfield 'Sea Spinner'. A two-piece, 8½ feet, hollow glass rod with spigot ferrule. Universal winch fittings on a fully-corked handle. This rod handles 8-14 lbs. line, spinning, float fishing or used as an ultra-light boat rod for the smaller species.

4. Winfield 'Salt Fisher'. A light boat rod in solid glass fibre. Two pieces with heavy-duty intermediate rings and single roller tip ring. 6½ feet long, the rod is intended for use with a multiplying reel. Use with 25-35 lbs. lines.

5. Winfield 'Pier Fisher'. Made in solid glass to withstand the strains of pier fishing. 7 feet long with a locking winch fitting and heavy duty rings. For 30-50 lbs. lines.

6. Winfield 'Tope Fisher'. A 6½ feet rod for the big fish. Solid glass tip and detachable locking handle. Double-roller tip and first intermediate ring. Will handle lines from 45 to 55 lbs. B/S Gimbal butt fitting to the handle.

7. Winfield 'Levelwind'. A metal-spooled trolling reel of 1/0 size. The line is laid evenly and automatically as the reel handle is turned. Gear ratio 1-2.75. Weight 15 ounces. Capacity 270 yards of 20 lbs. monofilament.

8. Winfield 'Beach Fisher'. A large-capacity ball-bearing fixed-spool reel for the shore-fisher. Capacity 250 yards of 25 lbs. nylon. Gear ratio 1-3.5. Weight 20 ounces.

9. Winfield 'Tope Fisher'. A large-capacity boat-fishing multiplier with metal spool. 3/0 size, it will hold 350 yards of 30 lbs. nylon. Weight 20 ounces. Gear ratio 1-2.4.

10. Winfield 'Saltfisher'. A boat-fishing multiplier with metal spool for 250 yards of 30 lbs. nylon line. Weighing 20 ounces, it has a gear ratio of 1-2.3. Size 2/0.

11. Winfield 'Surf Caster'. A light-weight plastic-spooled multiplier suitable for the bass fisherman. Weight 12½ ounces. Capacity 165 yards of 36 lbs. nylon. Gear ratio 1-2.92. The narrow spool allows good control during the cast.

12. Winfield 'Shore Caster'. A large-capacity reel with a plastic light-weight spool for the beach fisherman. 250 yards of 36 lbs. nylon. Weight 14 ounces. Gear ratio 1-2.92.

Chapter 9
Fly fishing

A FORM of angling that conjures up visions of a tweed-clad figure in a deer-stalker hat fishing a well stocked and very private chalkstream in the South of England. Fly fishing was, and is still thought to be, a rich man's sport. Nonsense . . . on the Yorkshire streams you are likely to meet up with the mill worker fishing the upstream wet fly on his day off and on the vast Midland reservoirs it is the car industry employee seen casting a long line to the big brownies and rainbows of the reservoirs.

Fly fishing as with most forms of angling knows no social barriers, it is undertaken and enjoyed by peers and postmen! True it is different and slightly exclusive, but this is because fly fishers have very few species to fish for and have developed a terminology of their own.

How does it differ from other types of freshwater angling? Well, the casting is vastly different, the rods are light in weight as they are constantly in use. The baits used are extremely light, they are made of feathers, fur and other almost weightless substances yet have to be put out onto the water so the weight is carried in the fly line.

The illustration left explains the basic movements in casting a fly with a single-handed rod. We will start with the line extended upon the water as it is easier to explain the breakdown of action from that position. As you will see the rod is held at position (a), the rod is then lifted, slowly at first and then gathering momentum until with a sharp flip the

line is lifted from the water and curls back over the head of the angler. Do not allow the rod to pass the position (b). This can be aided by ensuring that your thumb is firmly placed along the top of the cork handle. The line will take time to travel through the air and straighten behind you. It is a good thing to practise casting over grass watching the line uncurling at the end of the backcast. As soon as the line has straightened the rod is brought forward slowly at first and again quickening into a sharp flick at about position (c). This sharp movement will speed the travel of the fly line giving it sufficient air speed to throw the line forward (d), unroll the tip of the fly line

A typical chalk-stream of the South of England. Lush plant growth and richness of animal life provide excellent food for big trout.

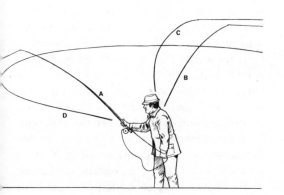

The correct grip for a single-handed fly rod.

A brown trout from a Midlands reservoir.

Fig. 1

and carry the fly cast on so that the line and cast are fully extended.

Obviously this type of casting takes a fair amount of practice to perfect but it is by no means as difficult as some people imagine. Terry Thomas, a man who has spent a great deal of his life teaching all manner of folk to cast a fly, often demonstrates that a line can be cast with one's feet providing the mechanics of the system have been studied and practised. Begin your practising by stripping off about twenty-five feet of line' and laying it out on the lawn; make certain that you have a clear backcast and that there is no possibility of striking anybody behind you with the line as it can inflict a nasty lash. It is good practice to attach a small piece of cloth tied on to represent the fly, to the end of the cast. This cast can be bought already tied in a tapered fashion and having a loop formed so that the fly line can be knotted to it. It is not a good system to attach a fly cast in this way. The knot is bulky and will catch in slender rod rings and when being retrieved it will cause a wash as the knot is drawn through the water. Far better to attach the cast to a permanent nylon length that has been previously spliced to the fly line with a needle knot (fig. 1). About a yard in length, of 18 lbs. B/S nylon, it will last for quite a time and will run through the rings without snagging and also cause practically no disturbance pulling the line through the water.

As I said, you can buy your casts but it is quite easy to tie them in a spare moment. A good length is two yards and this can be made by joining three equal pieces of nylon using double-blood knots. For river fishing where one could expect to find average trout, with the occasional big fellow, a cast formed from 12 lbs. to 8 lbs. and down to 5 lbs. B/S at the point would be right. Particularly so if the river is snaggy in nature. Open water situations, where the trout can be played clear of weed and other vegetation calls for a cast ending in a finer point, say 3 or 3.5 lbs. B/S. Where trout are educated or take only small flies an even finer point size must be fished, 4X which is approximately 2.5 lbs. breaking strain.

I am aware that some tackle manufacturers still insist upon using X sizes on their labelling. This can be confusing to the newcomer, so I include a table of ▶

Red Spinner   **March Brown**   **Wickham's Fancy**   **Pheasant Tail**

Coch-Y-Bondhu   **Black Spider**   **Red Tag**   **Greenwell's Glory**

Wickham's Fancy   **Tup's Indispensable**   **Red Quill**   **Greenwell's Glory**

Coachman   **Cinnamon Sedge**   **Gold Ribbed Hare's Ear**   **Sherry Spinner**

DRY FLIES

Wickham's Fancy *This fly can be tied to fish wet or dry and as a dry fly may be winged or hackled.*

Tup's Indispensable *A fly that is tied with a wide variety of dressings. It simulates the pale wateries but is useful as a fair representation of many live species. Possibly the best of the early season patterns.*

Red Quill *A standard pattern for all waters, whether running or still. The artificial does not closely resemble any natural insect.*

Greenwell's Glory *A killing pattern that can be fished wet or dry on rivers and lakes.*

Coachman *A fancy fly that has no counterpart in nature. It will take trout on running or still water and is an effective pattern when fished in the half-light of dusk.*

Cinnamon Sedge *A fly to be used from mid-summer through to the end of the season. The natural sedge hatches in large numbers on the rivers of this country and the lakes of Wales and Ireland.*

Gold Ribbed Hare's Ear *A first-rate fly for trout and grayling. It is said to be a fancy fly but trout recognize it as a medium olive in the spring. Many people fish the pattern wingless to simulate the hatching nymph.*

Sherry Spinner *A middle-of-the-season fly that represents the female blue-winged olive spinner. Best fished just before dusk.*

WET FLIES

Red Spinner *A standard pattern that has been used by trout fishermen for two centuries. This fly represents the female spinner of the olive dun.*

March Brown *One of the most popular flies for the rough, fast-flowing streams. It is rarely seen, as a live insect, on still water and is best used in the early part of the season.*

Wickham's Fancy *A fancy fly that does not represent any particular insect. Originating on the chalk-streams of the South of England, it will take trout, sea trout, grayling and coarse fish that rise to a fly.*

Pheasant Tail *A truly universal fly representing a wide variety of natural insects. Useful on lakes as well as running water for trout and grayling.*

Coch-Y-Bondhu *A Welsh pattern tied to represent a small beetle. It is a popular fly and can be a killing lure on the small streams and lakes of western and northern areas of the country.*

Black Spider *W. C. Stewart's favourite wet fly, said to be among the finest of patterns for early-season fishing.*

Red Tag *The standard wet fly for grayling, although it is also a fine pattern for taking trout. Most commonly fished in the northern counties.*

Greenwell's Glory *The best known of all trout wet flies that imitates a number of olive duns. The fame and use of this pattern has spread throughout the world.*

These are all wet flies . . . but what a difference in size! The two largest are reservoir lures; in the middle are examples of conventional lake flies. The small flies are of the type used by Northern anglers on the tiny moorland becks and streams.

the approximate relative breaking strains.

1X	7 lbs. B/S	3X	3.5 lbs. B/S
2X	5 lbs. B/S	4X	2.5 lbs. B/S
		5X	1.5 lbs. B/S

I have given a method for tying a cast suitable for fishing a single fly. This is correct for dry-fly fishing and I believe that it is sound advice when I say to beginners that they should become competent casters before attempting to fish more than one wet fly on the cast.

A word about the rod and the reel. I only fish fly on small streams and rivers so an 8½ feet rod light and easy on the wrist is my choice. It is made of hollow glass, with a glass spigot ferrule and throws an AFTM No. 6 line. This is a line of a weight balanced to the casting ability of the type of rod used. The formula by

A plump brown trout from an Irish limestone lake.

Fly fishing on a typical mountain stream.

which the manufacturers arrive at the best weight is quite complicated and best left to them to decide upon. The line has a built-in forward taper along its length, this aids the essential turn-over of the line and fly to settle the lure gently on the water with the minimum of disturbance. Lines are made to float or to sink after casting. You will have noticed that the word disturbance crops up at regular intervals in this chapter, this is because trout are sensitive fish and are easily frightened by unnecessary splashing. Any attention to tackle and presentation of the fly is of the utmost importance if you wish to become a successful fly-fisher.

The reel is not all that important in fly fishing . . . it is only really a means of storing line. All but the biggest fish can be played by allowing a trout to take line after hooking, and letting the line run through the fingers. As he weakens so line is stripped back through the rod rings with the left hand and allowed to fall at one's feet. Ensure that the reel capacity is large enough to accommodate the fly line and about fifty yards of nylon or braided Terylene backing . . . this will be used if the fish is large and strips more than your fly line from the reel. Reservoir trout are often bigger than their river-dwelling relatives, so a backing of 100 yards or more may be necessary. I am not going to discuss this form of trout fishing as the book is intended for the beginner and reservoir fishing is a sport for the advanced angler of better than average casting ability.

There are two types of trout fly fishing and two distinct types of fly. First the wet fly. As its name suggests it is fished wet or rather under the water-surface. It is intended to represent either a small fish or as is more usual an insect. A fly is a member of the Ephemeridae or similar group that is making its way from the bottom of the lake or river. Here it has spent early life as an egg, then a larva and soon to emerge from the juvenile stage to become a fully winged fly. The appearance of these insects on the water is called a hatch and it is at this time that the trout reap a rich harvest. They feed avidly on those insects coming to the surface and so we anglers fish an artificial fly to them in mid-water. The number of patterns are many, too many to mention here, so I have given on the illustration the name of the fly, the natural species it is tied to represent and a guide to its use. Generally wet flies are fished progres-

sively over an area that the angler expects will hold a trout. Sometimes, if fortunate, he will have seen his fish but more often he will be fishing to known lies. The wet fly can be cast upstream allowing the fly to drift down at the speed of the current. This is good practice because trout always lie facing upstream so the fly will travel down and over their heads. For the learner it may be difficult to maintain contact with the cast. The usual fashion is to cast across the stream letting the fly swing round in the current thereby covering an arc of travel. An offer, as the bite of a game fish is often called, will be felt as a gentle plucking or pull at the line. There must be an instant reaction on the part of the fisherman. A quick lift of the rod tip and the trout is on! You will feel the urgent movements of the fish through both the rod and the line, which is all the time held in the fingers of the left hand. Play it gently, give line to the sudden dashes and recover line quickly if the fish moves towards you. It is essential to keep in direct contact maintaining a tight line. As the fish tires trap the line under the first finger of the rod hand, reach round on to your belt for the landing net, extend it and by lifting the rod tip lead the trout over the rim and into the net.

In stillwater there is no current to work the flies around and across a stream, so it is a job for the angler. After casting and giving the fly time to sink in the water it has to be stripped back by pulling line through the rings with the left hand.

Difficult but satisfying—fly fishing in a tiny brook. The trout are small but put up a hard fight when lured from beneath overhanging trees and other lies.

Lough Derg, on the River Shannon, has huge trout that are taken on fly and spinner.

79

Jack Austin fly fishing on a small trout stream in Hampshire.

I cannot say just how fast one should retrieve the fly. It depends on the taking mood of the fish and the depth at which they are feeding. A slow stripping of the line will allow the fly to fish deep and vice-versa. Fishing a deep-sunk fly will necessitate using a sinking line, it does not weigh any more than the floating line of equivalent number but does not have the little buoyancy bubbles along its length that the floater has.

A dry fly is made to float. It will sit on the surface film of the water supported by the stiff hackle fibres. Quite often a silicone spray is applied to ensure that the fly continues to float. Dry flies represent the adult insect drying its wings before flying off to mate or as the spent insect that has returned to the water to lay the eggs and then die. The fly is fished in a more positive way, not just cast to cover water area but to a definite fish. Look for one that has been seen to rise, dimpling the surface as it takes a natural fly. The dry-fly fisher will walk the bank searching for fish in a feeding mood, he casts above the fish so that the fly drifts down in a lifelike way, covering the spot where the rising fish was last seen.

To be successful, a dry-fly man must study the natural flies that are hatching and if possible fish an artificial pattern that will fool the trout. Casting and presentation of the fly on the water should be delicate, without slapping the line or splashing with the fly. Once put down, a trout will be very wary about rising again for some time.

The natural fly, a sedge, or, as it is sometimes called, caddis fly. On this day there was great activity as the trout took the natural insect from the surface of Lough Ennel.

The man-made fly, tied from materials which accurately copied the live sedge. Tied on a number 8 hook to produce an artificial of about the same size as its live counterpart.

A trout rises to the fly, fished on a slow-sinking line just below the surface of the lough.

The rod arcs over and absorbs the wild lunges of the trout at close quarters. It is important that a fish is not brought to the net too early in the fight.

With the landing net rim sunk below the water, the fish is gently drawn towards and over the rim.

The fish, a lake trout of 5 lbs. from the shallows of Lough Ennel. The point of the hook can be seen protruding from the fleshy upper jaw. 81

Chapter 10
Introduction to the sea

SEA fishing is the fastest-growing branch of the sport of angling. Being an island race we are fortunate in having comparatively easy access to saltwater no matter where we dwell. The sea can never be more than a hundred miles from home. Sea angling is free, apart from dues payable when fishing from a pier or hiring a boat to fish offshore. There is no closed season, although the fish in their migratory habits impose fishing seasons upon us.

The natural elements play a much greater role in determining where and when we can fish in the sea. Wind is the major problem. Gales far out from our shores can build up monumental seas which keep boat fishers ashore and, at times, beach anglers at home. We need the wind, though cursed at times it may be, for it creates currents out in the oceans which move the mass of minute life, known as plankton, and bring it close in to the shores of Britain. This, in turn, brings the fish. The life cycle or food chain of most of our sea fishes is quite simple to understand. Fish spawn, releasing their eggs into the sea, plants loose spores or seeds into the currents and together these minute forms of life drift and grow in the upper layers of the water. The sun with its heat provides warmth, oxygen is taken in from the air and the trace minerals necessary for these small organisms are constantly washed out from the land mass.

The plant or phyto-plankton grows and feeds the zoo or animal plankton.

Small fishes then eat their share of both and in turn are eaten by larger fish like the herring. Vast shoals of herring, of which we as human beings consume many, are preyed upon by even larger fish, notably members of the cod family. At the end of the food chain are the main predators, the sharks, tunny and whales which are of course aquatic mammals.

We as anglers are not concerned with the fish life of the open sea. Fishing for us starts at the water's edge and continues out to depths of up to 50 fathoms or so. It is between these boundary lines that angling species can live, feed on the available animal life and be fairly easily reached.

Tides — and their influence

Sea anglers have to contend with another form of water movement, tide. Normally two high tides and two periods of low water occur in each day of twenty-four hours. They are neither regular in strength nor in appearance at particular times of day. Springs or high tides are brought about by the gravitational pull of the moon being at its greatest. Exceptionally high spring tides occur when both the sun and the moon are having a similar effect. Neap tides are a direct reversal of this situation. We need not have to make complicated calculations regarding tides and their effect on a day's fishing because most coastal towns have a tide table published for the immediate area and the Admiralty provides yearly predictions, for all British

Mackerel Scomber scombus

Scad or horse mackerel Trachurus trachurus

sea areas, of tide height and strength.

As anglers all we need to know is whether there will be sufficient water to float the angling boat or to find a large enough depth of water to bring fish within casting range. Tide can have an influence on the feeding habits of our quarry, certainly exceptionally high tides are difficult to fish as too much lead is required to hold the bottom with the bait and often fish do not feed whilst the stream is at its strongest. A weak neap tide often creates the circumstance where fish will not take a bait, a lack of current slows up the flow of natural feed to them so they lie dormant waiting for the tide to run before becoming active.

There are no hard and fast rules about fish behaviour or feeding patterns, what I have written is very much a generalisation. Conditions will differ and are best learned by experience or talking to local anglers about it.

The salinity or saltiness of the water can be an influence on the type of species that one can expect in a given area. Fish such as bass, mullet and flounders are tolerant of a high content of fresh or brackish water. Bass, though, would prefer the freshwater to be clean and free from large amounts of mud or silt in suspension.

Examples of fishing ground and associated species

There are too many species of fish, likely to be caught by sea anglers, for me to mention them in great detail. This is, after all, a book intended for newcomers so I will consider the types of fishing ground and discuss those species that we are likely to come upon.

Flat bottom

There must be more of this type of ground around our coasts than any other. Sometimes there will be hard sand as a base, or mud, shingle, shell and perhaps a mixture of all four. If the water is shallow a prolific weed growth can provide both cover for the fish and a habitat for smaller animals on which the fish can feed. Beds of shellfish are wonderful angling marks, food for the fish and a holding ground to which anglers can return with the knowledge that there can be fish at most times. Where this habitat exists it is called a *mark* and one of this type would be the mussel beds off Folkestone, Kent, renowned for plaice. This species of flatfish (fig. 1) is fond of the mussel but will take lugworms as a hookbait (fig. 2).

Broken ground

Often found under the base of cliffs but also far out where undersea cliffs and ledges have eroded. The base material can be sand, mud or just smaller stones. Crabs, lobsters and other shellfish live in among the broken ground together with an enormous variety of invertebrate life. If in shallow water bass, pollack, codling and wrasse would feed here and in deeper water skate and

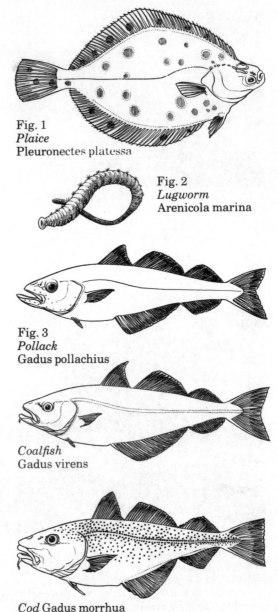

Fig. 1
Plaice
Pleuronectes platessa

Fig. 2
Lugworm
Arenicola marina

Fig. 3
Pollack
Gadus pollachius

Coalfish
Gadus virens

Cod Gadus morrhua

It is all broken ground off the 'Old Man of Hoy', Orkney.

other large species would predominate.

Reefs and pinnacle rocks

Many cliffs and rocky peninsulas are to be found around Britain. A number of them do not finish at the water's edge but continue out under the waves sometimes for many miles. As a range of mountains has a number of peaks so these reefs also have an undulating pattern to their tops. Such underwater configuration provides homes, breeding areas and reasonable security for the

obstruction to the tidal stream and currents, food is often swept to them and gathers, as in a larder, around the edges. Consequently many small species dwell on a reef and this in turn attracts a wide variety of the larger brethren.

Pinnacle rocks are normally found out in deeper water where they can rise, sharply, almost to the surface from great depths. Different species are found and hooked at different depths when fishing these grounds. Figure 4 gives a rough indication of some of the species and depths at which I have found them to be. Many fishermen will tell you that the greater the depth of water the larger the fish. This statement, relative to species, is true. And there is no better fishing ground than a pinnacle rock.

Offshore sandbanks

We have a number of these fishing marks in the South of England which are a source of embarrassment to navi-

Many reefs and pinnacle rocks do not show above the surface at any stage of the tide. These rocks, off Achill Head, Co. Mayo, show through all but the very highest spring tides. This is a serious consideration when attempting to place the boat for rod and line fishing.

species that choose to live there. Pollack and coalfish are two such fish; from an identification point they are similar so I show the differences (fig. 3).

Because these reefs form a natural

Fig. 5
This is an echo-sounder trace of The Shambles Bank, off Portland Bill. The bank rises out of 90 feet of water up to a peak at 45 feet. The view is foreshortened because of the speed of the boat over the ground. This portion of the trace represents a length of 1½ miles.

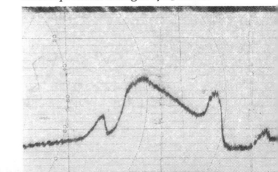

gating officers of the many ships that pass through the channel and out to the Atlantic! Happily, they are well charted and buoyed. A sandbank supports a varied animal life, sandeels and worms predominate and are of interest to sea fishers (fig. 5). Fairly fast tides rip around and over these banks and the action of the current is to scour small creatures from the sand. Lying in the lee of the banks and sheltered from the full force of the current we can expect to find turbot (fig. 6) and other flatfish. These species may seem ungainly and at a disadvantage in fast water, but they can flatten themselves against or even bury themselves in the sand and avoid the pressure. From this position they lie in wait to pounce on fish and worms swept over the bank to their waiting mouths.

Estuaries

Here we have a situation where tidal flow will have a marked effect on the species found. Brackish water will determine the type of fish that we find here. As I have said already bass (fig. 7) and mullet will swim well up into a river, so will flounders (fig. 8) and sometimes codling. A vast quantity of food will be swept down on the freshwater flow to be met by the saltwater coming in on the tide. As the flow of one meets and becomes equal to the other this food will be deposited on the bottom and it is there that fish will come, and anglers ought to be! I know that many of you will say that saltwater has a different specific gravity to that of freshwater and that there will

The bass fishers' dream, four rolling breakers at Inch, Co. Kerry, and not an angler in sight!

Fig. 4

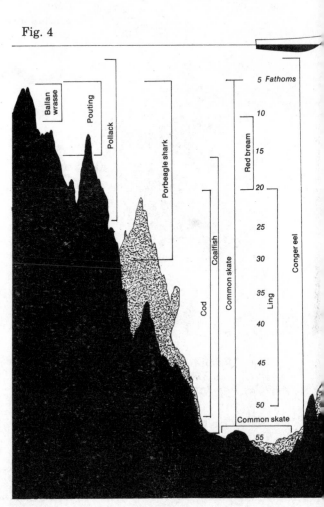

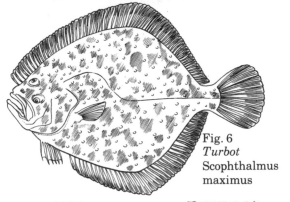

Fig. 6
Turbot
Scophthalmus
maximus

Fig. 7 *Kevin Linnane, sea angling officer with the Inland Fisheries Trust, with a fine bass of 8 lbs. from Inch Strand.*

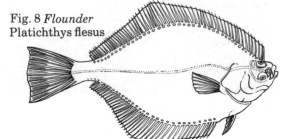

Fig. 8 *Flounder*
Platichthys flesus

be an over-riding action. This is true but the disturbance, often seen as a *boil* on the top of the water, will draw fish onto feed.

Shingle beaches

Dungeness must rate as the classical example of this type of fishing mark. The strong sweeping action over centuries of channel tides has resulted in a spur of shingle jutting out into the sea. As the current is forced to curve around the end of this spur it has formed a deep scour in the sand off the end of the steep-to beach. It is in this scour that anglers endeavour to cast their baits, for here food gathers and so too do the fish. Dungeness is too well known to dwell upon further, but remember that there are many similar shorefishing situations in Britain. A great number of them will fish as well if not better now that so many anglers are fishing from the shingle.

Storm beaches

The name is almost synonymous with one species—bass. Storm beaches are so called because they fish well after a storm has created a swell far offshore. This ends as a towering surf that crashes down on the sand forcing worms, sandeels and other minute life from their homes. Most of these beaches are to be found on the south-west to north-west facing shores of these islands. The day after a stiff sou-west blow will find the surf fining down to three or four feet in height with breakers rolling into the

beach. It is then that the bass and some flatfish will move into the surf to look for the food that they know has been forced from the sand. These fish may well be followed in by predators, such as the spurdog and tope (fig. 9).

Piers

At practically every seaside town there is a pier. Most of them allow fishermen to use the facilities available. Pier fishing can be said to be two things; on a short pier it allows people to fish in relatively deep water without having to be good casters and on a long pier it becomes boat fishing as the angler is so far offshore. Most inshore species can be taken whilst fishing piers and jetties but remember the gear will have to be strong enough to play a fish and then haul it vertically up to the fishing platform. Some pier anglers equip themselves with a dropnet which they lower to the water and sink below the hooked fish. The net is then pulled up taking the strain from the rod and line. As there are often cafes and restaurants on these structures the fish come to expect kitchen waste to be thrown into the sea. A useful form of groundbaiting so try fishing as near to the kitchen door as possible!

How to seek fish

Fish will not be found spread evenly over the sea bed. They inhabit an area because it has something that they require to support life. Security, food, somewhere to breed and even somewhere to escape the constant pressure of current and wave action. You will, of course, take fish on the open ground, where they may have ventured for the food that is there. Or they may be on a migratory path which takes them close to your fishing mark.

Anything that forms an obstruction to the movement of the water is a potential angling mark; a patch of rocks, old piles and breakwaters, a wreck, a gully formed by the tide, warm-water outlet pipes from power stations on the coast, pipes from factories that discharge edible waste, the list is endless. Try everything but keep a diary if you can, noting down important details such as time of day, tide height and whether it is flooding or ebbing, the tackle and the bait that was successful. To catch fish regularly it is always so necessary to come to learn something about them and their habits.

Fig. 9
Tope
Eugaleus galeus

The longest pier in the world, at Southend on Sea. Regular fishing contests are held on its 1¼ miles of fishing platforms.

Chapter 11
Boat fishing:
tackle and baits

THE title of this chapter conjures up so many visions. Fishing far out at sea for huge specimen conger over the wrecks, paddling a tiny stem dinghy up a West Country river estuary whilst trolling for bass, a big game boat with extended outriggers trailing feathered lures for fish of a thousand pounds or a weekend fishing trip for whiting off the coast of Northumberland. It is all boat fishing but could any sport be so diverse? The link between all these examples of sea angling is that some men, and newcomers at that, can engage in it. Boat fishing has an attraction for the British angler that is hard to define. Being an island race may have something to do with it but there is also the lure of the huge fish and a desire to tangle with something larger than oneself.

Because boat fishing can be done in so many ways I will deal with the fish and their habitat rather than how one gets to them. Boats are made in different shapes and sizes to work under differing conditions of wind and sea, very rarely are they designed for sea angling. Where there is a specific need for a particular choice of boat I will mention it.

At one time rods for boat angling were stiff, stoutly-built poles that gave fish little chance to display their fighting qualities, nor did they give the sea angler much pleasure in using them. With the arrival of glass fibre coupled with the availability of synthetic lines, sea angling took on a new look. Fishermen began to balance their tackle to the

fish and to the elements.

I use three rods for my boat fishing. Each of them will do a definite job which is to handle and balance to a breaking strain of line and a range of weights of fish. Due allowance will be given for the water conditions and method of angling when choosing which rod to fish with on the day. All rods are constructed from glass fibre. It withstands the wear and tear of boat angling and is not affected by salt water. The rod rings and other fittings are strong and suitable for use by the sea.

Rods for boat fishing

I suppose the first rod that boat fishermen will buy is a general-purpose rod. The inference from the name is that it will cope with most fishing situations with the possible exception of handling really big fish. This may well be true if we understand that the rod will not break. But will there be any pleasure in using such a rod? The basic requirements for a good rod are few in number. It should be of sound design and manufacture. The line strength for the rod should be stated as near as is possible. The rod must be as light in the hands as can be achieved because it will have to be held almost constantly and, of course, it must give the maximum amount of sensitivity in use.

Let us look at the light tackle rod for small fish in slack tide conditions. Best made in hollow fibreglass, such a rod would be slightly longer than is normal

A roller tip ring for a light boat rod. This type of ring is intended for use when fishing a multiplying reel, above the rod.

for a boat rod. Eight feet long in two pieces, either with a spigot joint dividing the rod into equal halves or a tip of 5 feet and a handle section of 3 feet, and about a 2 lb. test curve allowing the use of 10 lbs. line. With this rod we can fish for flats and other small fish with a couple of ounces of lead. If a bigger specimen comes to the hook there is sufficient length in the rod to absorb the strain. If tidal strength is more than a knot or so a heavier lead is called for to hold bottom.

Now consider the next class of rod which comes into the general-purpose category. This is a shorter rod, about $6\frac{1}{2}$-7 feet in length. It can be of hollow or solid glass construction and is usually in two pieces with the working tip slotted into the handle section. This rod will handle lines from 25 lbs. to 35 lbs. and fish lead up to a pound. Fish of 40-50 lbs. would be well within the capabilities of the blank. I must make it quite clear that I am writing about fish that cannot make themselves fast, conger in a wreck or big common skate on the bottom. These would present a different problem demanding a stronger rod and line.

The third rod in the group is stouter in build, about the same length as the general-purpose rod but with a test curve of 15 lbs., which will fish a line of 50 lbs. breaking strain. This type of blank will handle the big skate, conger and shark up to 150 lbs.

There can be a case made for heavier rods for the larger sharks, but this type of fishing is outside the scope of this book.

An ultra-light boat rod, fishing a 14 lbs. line, arcs into a shallow-water cod.

The conger eel, Conger conger, can at first sight be confused with the ling. Congers have an undivided dorsal fin, whilst the ling has two dorsal fins and a barbel under the chin.

89

The author with a skate of 100 lbs. taken from the broken ground.

Fig. 1 *Kidney harness*

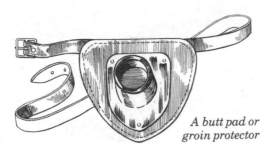

A butt pad or groin protector

Reels

There are two types suitable for use with boat rods, the multiplier and the centre-pin or single-action reel as it is often called. The fixed-spool reel does not have a place in boat fishing except perhaps when spinning from the boat.

In choosing the type of reel you wish to use it is necessary to consider several factors.

A. The breaking strain of the line as matched to the rod.

B. The amount of line that is required on the spool; this is determined by the depths in which you will fish and whether the fish will run and possibly strip off large amounts of line.

C. Whether you wish to fish the reel above or below the rod.

Multiplier	*Centre-pin*
A. Good. The multiplier can handle all but the finest lines —has clutch control for delicate adjustment.	A. Average. Rarely has a clutch device. Is more suited to lines above 20 lbs. for boat fish.
B. Carries fair amount of line with moderate retrieve.	B. Very large line capacity and fast retriever.
C. Above the rod.	C. Below the rod

Multipliers work on the principle that when lowering the tackle the reel is flipped out of gear and the spool is then free to turn. When retrieving line one turn of the handle will turn the spool two, three or, on some reels, four turns. The reel can be set to a known drag by manipulation of the star drag control; if a strong fish pulls on the line at a strain above this setting the spool will slip, allowing the fish to take line from the reel. It is a form of slipping clutch of great value to the angler. This reel has to be fished above the rod and is often available in left or right-handed models. The larger multipliers have fittings which enable a kidney or full shoulder harness to be worn (fig. 1).

Centre-pin reels are simple in construction and in use. The spool is carried on a bearing set at right angles to the rod. It revolves freely in both directions. When lowering the terminal tackle the spool is allowed to turn with the right hand cupping the rim of the spool to control the speed of drop. Line is brought back by simply winding the reel in the opposite direction. Some models have a form of slipping clutch that allows line to be pulled from the spool without turning the handles of the reel. Unfortunately most centre-pins do not have this feature, which means that a fish that runs strongly can strip line from the spool which, in turn, sets the handles revolving madly. If you happen to put fingers in the way they could be rapped sharply or even broken. Due to the fairly large diameter of these reels they have both a big line capacity and fast rate of retrieve. Whereas most multipliers are made of synthetic substances, plastic end plates with metal spools and fittings, there are still a number of centre-pins in wood, although there are a few models using metal or Tufnol in their construction. The important thing is that all reels used in salt water should be as near corrosion proof as possible, both internally and externally. Clean your reels regularly and lubricate them to the manufacturers' instructions. A little care after each fishing trip will help to give the reel a long and trouble-free life.

Lines and their uses

Your line is the most important piece of tackle, if one can call line tackle. After all, you can fish without a rod or reel and hand-lining was and still is a most successful method of fishing. A line has to serve two purposes: to get the bait down to the fish and, if lucky, to get up to the surface whatever has taken the offering.

Let us consider the problem first of getting the bait to the fish. Most sea fishing is done in some considerable depth of water and with a further pressure playing a part . . . that of tide. This inevitably means that the line and bait have to be given the assistance of a lead or some form of weight to take them down to the bottom. All lines, however fine in diameter, set up a resistance to the tide. So using any particular breaking strain of the materials available becomes a compromise between a line and rod, light enough to be used with the minimum size of lead to allow fishing the bottom effectively and with sensitivity and a line strong enough to bring a good fish up to the boat. A further factor is that one's line should always match the power of the rod used. To overload a rod with a line that is of a far too heavy breaking strain for the power curve achieved with the rod under load will mean that you will be unable to break out a snagged lead from the ground and any heavy fish strong enough to fully compress the rod will produce a condition of stalemate. Any rod that is compressed beyond a curve resembling a right-angle has no power. Obviously in such a situation the answer is to use a heavier rod, matching the line, which will curve over in an arc and then attempt to straighten itself. It is this spring in a rod, combined with a pumping action from the angler, which beats a fish.

On the other hand, using a line that is too light for the rod will create the situation where using maximum pressure and pumping action will break the line. Taking *light tackle* fishing to the extreme, where fish are regularly breaking the angler, is unnecessary and unsporting. There is nothing clever in leaving a trail of fish swimming in the sea with a string of tackle attached to their mouths!

Rods used to be labelled as having this or that test curve. At best this is an arbitrary method of assessing the capabilities of any particular rod. Today, more and more manufacturers are stating that a rod is balanced for use with a definite breaking strain of line . . . altogether a much better system of labelling and of great assistance to the tyro angler.

I stated earlier that there were a number of lines one could use for sea fishing. All have advantages and, naturally, disadvantages. Monofilament nylon is probably the most popular line, chiefly because it is a lot cheaper than other materials. It can be made in much finer breaking strains than any braided line and with care will last almost indefinitely. The main drawback is that it stretches under pressure, possibly up to ten per cent of its original length. This can bring about two problems. One is a lack of contact between angler and fish as the tremor of the bite is felt. Even a vigorous strike may not succeed in hooking the fish because this inherent elasticity absorbs

the strike action. The other is that winding a line back on to the reel under considerable strain produces a pressure on the spool which will in the case of a plastic spool burst it. With a metal spool it may force the side flanges outwards until they contact the side-plates and lock the reel solid.

Nevertheless it is a good material to make a line from and, provided that a little attention is given to observing just two golden rules, trouble should not occur. Firstly, before winding on nylon line to your reel, wind on about four layers of braided backing line. Being softer it will absorb most of the build-up of line pressure from the nylon. Secondly, try to use a positive pumping action, winding in the line on the downward stroke when much less line pressure will build up. When bottom fishing with heavy gauges of monofilament nylon never use a reel with a plastic spool.

Braided Terylene lines are becoming increasingly popular. They are a little more expensive than nylon but do not suffer from the stretch problem. Obviously this can be of real value when striking a bite. It also enables an angler to keep in contact with a fish that *runs*; tope, and shark particularly, will move off at speed and sometimes double-back and run in towards the boat. To be able to retrieve line quickly and feel, through the line, a positive contact with the fish in its efforts to escape will aid one's chance of landing it.

Unfortunately, breaking strains being

equal, braided lines are larger in diameter than monofilament nylon. Therefore, when bottom fishing in a tidal flow, they require a larger lead to effectively hold the ground. Also a little more care is necessary when using them as braided lines are prone to abrasion, either from rough rod rings and guides or below-surface hazards such as rocks, the keel of the fishing boat and even the rough skin of certain species of fish. The diligent angler will guard against these hazards when using the material, but it can be a problem. Personally I favour the use of braided line; most of the pitfalls one encounters can be overcome and the direct contact the line gives more than makes up for them.

As I said before, no matter what the line in use there will be a pressure sweeping the line downtide. Some of this can be overcome with the judicious use of the right amount of lead. But there are conditions where the lead required to hold bottom will make fishing difficult and contact with the end tackle well-nigh impossible. I can bring to mind a situation when fishing the Straits of Gibraltar, where two pounds of lead was almost floating on the surface! The tide was more than fierce, it was ridiculous. The answer was to use a line which had only recently arrived on the angling scene: Monel metal wire line, single strand and immensely strong with, of course, its own in-built weight. The advantage, on that occasion, was that I was able to use a pound of lead, where previously I couldn't get

bottom, let alone hold it! The problem is that being fairly stiff this wire tends to spring off the reel in coils if it is not tightly wound on to the reel. This necessitates a constant attention to what you are doing when retrieving line. Also, if the wire breaks or you attempt to pull out a lead that is lodged in the rough ground it can act just like a cheese cutter. The effects of which can be very nasty!

The last of the four materials is a compromise line known as lead-cored braided line that has its own weight running through a hollow braided Terylene or Dacron. Gone are the dangers of a line breakage, as with wire line, but naturally there is a penalty to be paid. It is that because of the lead core and the increased diameter of a braided make-up this line is a good deal thicker, in cross-section, than the previous three lines written about. However, using the line can be an advantage over normal braided line when fishing the bottom and it really comes into its own as a trolling line. For here the angler has always had to add weight, either in the form of a spiral lead or Wye lead, to get the line to fish the bait below the surface. With this type of line, carrying its own weight, a bait will troll more naturally because it does not have the dampening effect of a lead secured just in front it. In the diagram (fig. 2) I have attempted to show the theoretical curves adopted by each line, in tide, when using the same amount of lead to effectively hold the ground. It will be seen that, with a lessening in the belling effect,

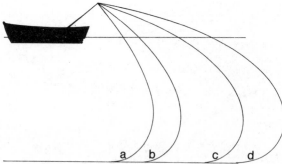

Fig. 2 *Theoretical curves for the four lines most commonly used by sea anglers. (a) Single-strand wire. (b) Lead-cored braided Terylene. (c) Monofilament nylon. (d) Braided Terylene or nylon.*

wire and lead-cored lines do have a place in sea angling.

I feel a point that should be made is that, as yet, only braided Terylene and Dacron lines are manufactured to meet the requirements of the International Game Fishing Association. Class line records, as they are called, can only be allowed when the fish has been taken on a line which conforms to their specification. Open records can, of course, be claimed when using almost any line.

*Jams for Terylene and Dacron braided lines

These two modern materials, Terylene and Dacron, can be braided to form fishing line of immense strength. Because of the accuracy with which each of the individual strands of fibre that go together to form the braid is made, the strength in terms of breaking strain can be stated accurately. A braided class line of 30 lbs. breaking strain has to part at 27 lbs. pull and *it will*. When claiming a class line record for any fish a section of the line used has to be provided for inspection and testing by the International Game Fishing Association.

Lines are braided to produce either a solid braid or a hollow braid. There is no real difference in line strength or in diameter, but forming a loop in the hollow braid is far easier. The loop can be made by splicing the line back on itself using a splicing needle. A loop in the end of braided line can be extremely useful when game fishing. It is normal practice

to fish with a doubled leader. This can be up to 15 feet in length and serves to strengthen the line just back from the trace where most abrasion on the line will happen. Of course, this doubled leader in no way increases the line strength overall, so does not invalidate a claim for a class record.

Braided lines should never be knotted because of the strangulation of the fibres from which the line is made. Other methods of joining lines, forming loops and droppers had to be sought. The *Jammed Hangman's Knot* serves sea anglers well for this type of line. It is formed (fig. 3) by passing about 18 inches of line around a stick or some convenient fixed object. The free end is then twisted over and over the reel line for about 1½ inches. Take the end and bind tightly back over the twists for their entire length. Take care to make each coil of the binding even and tight over the twists. The free end of the braided line is then tied around the single strand to form a half-hitch. Then it is taken across to the other single strand and a further half-hitch tied. As a final security in your knot cut the loose end off to leave a piece about ½ inch long. This end can be sealed with the flame from a match or lighted cigarette. The hard knob of burned braid will prevent the line unravelling.

Another highly successful knot for braided lines, the *Policansky Knot*, was brought from the big-game fishing centre in Cape Town. Policansky, the man who designed the sea angling reels carrying

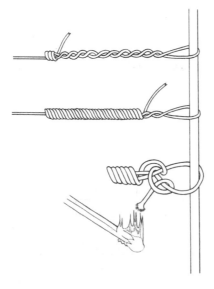

Fig. 3 *Jammed hangman's knot*

*'Terylene' is the registered trademark of I.C.I. Ltd. and 'Dacron' is the registered trademark of Du Pont's Polyester fibre.

94

his name, knows what is asked for in a knot. Many years fishing the waters around South Africa have taught him that the real danger with braided lines is that they will, under pressure, fail through abrasion. The constant rubbing of lines on metal connectors, such as swivels and links, can rub through the braid very quickly.

'Poly' came up with a knot to cure this. It works on the principle that the line retains a straight pull to the connector but is prevented from actually touching the metal by bindings wrapped around it. The tighter the knot is pulled the better it will perform. To make this knot pass the free end of the line through the eye of the swivel. Take it around the main line and bind the loop formed with the loose end. Make the bindings sit on the line as neatly and as tightly as you can. Finally, pass the loose end through the swivel eye and pull on the main line to draw the bindings tight. There is no need to secure the free end; it will stand tight but can be freed when the fishing day is over (fig. 4).

The various knots for nylon line used in sea angling are the same as are tied when coarse fishing. Examples of the knots and explanation of the tying methods are contained in Chapter 2.

Hooks

Choose your hook with care and regard to the size of both fish and bait. Cod and its close relatives have huge mouths, whereas flounders and other flatfish have comparatively small mouths. It is very easy to shroud the point of the hook with a massive portion of bait. Your strike may not set the hook because the force with which it is made can be easily absorbed by the bait. See that the point is sharp; a few minutes' attention with a hook hone will keep it keen and the barb not too rank. My choice is for a hook that is strong enough to hold the fish, not over large and as sharp as I can make it. Hooks are cheap, so only use them for one outing.

The patterns (fig. 5) are all good types for boat angling; the heavier irons, for shark, skate and conger eels. Types A

Fig. 5 *A range of sea-fishing hooks, shown two-thirds normal size.*

A. *An 8/0 Mustad Seamaster, tapered and brazed eye, flat forged, used for big fish, shark, tope, conger, skate and halibut.*
B. *A 6/0 Model Perfect, down-eyed in forged stainless steel. A good all-round hook for heavy boat fishing.*
C. *A 7/0 forged and tinned O'Shaughnessy hook for general fishing.*
D. *4/0 needle-eyed, forged stainless steel*

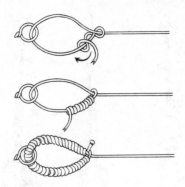

Fig. 4
Policansky knot

Tarpon hook. Immensely strong, though small in size.
E. *3/0 general-purpose hook for boat fishing.*
F. *3/0 long-shanked, fine wire Cannelle hook. A good iron for light fishing from the beach.*
G. *4/0 Kirby bend, fine wire, down-eyed and forged hook for beach and light boat angling.*
H. *2/0 Hollow point Beak hook, often called a baitholder hook. It is nickel plated and has two slices on the shank intended to prevent bait from sliding down on to the hook bend.*

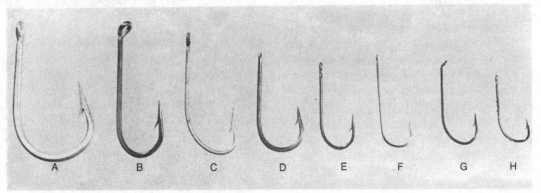

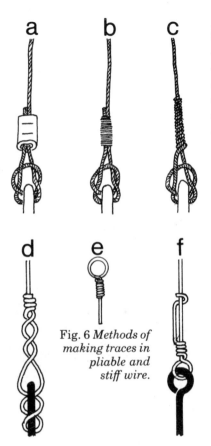

Fig. 6 *Methods of making traces in pliable and stiff wire.*

A selection of sea-angling swivels.
A. *Heavy-duty brass swivels can be had with a spiral link for trace or rig attachment.*
B. *Stainless steel, ball-bearing snap-link swivels used spinning or light trolling.*
C. *Three-way and ordinary box swivel.*
D. *Snap-link barrel swivels.*
E. *Three-way barrel swivel.*

and D have brazed round or needle eyes. These will be attached to wire traces using the special knots and fixing methods that have been developed to handle this trace material (fig. 6). Ordinary knots will not tie in wire; it is a lot less pliable than nylon. *a.* Shows how to fix the wire to the hook eye using a metal ferrule which is crimped onto the wire after the wire is passed through the hook eye twice. *b.* After the wire has been made fast to the hook eye. This method stops the wire from slipping by simply binding with fuse wire which is afterwards soldered. *c.* A method for making traces in fine wire, such as is used spinning or trolling. Nylon-covered wire is tied and twisted over as shown. The nylon covering is fused by holding over a lighted match. This is a reasonable way to make traces for light fishing, but I would not recom-

mend it for heavy fishing.

Making a shark hook fast to the trace is easy in soft pliable wire but sometimes we need a stiff single-strand wire to form a mount on which to place the bait fish. Use method *d* to tie on the hook with this material. *e.* Shows how to form an eye on the wire for pliable trace attachment. If you are a handyman it is quite easy to make a sound job of your hook fixing by using the method *f* which will not slip or unravel.

Swivels

Great stress is placed upon a swivel when fishing. Nylon can stretch and absorb undue strain but the swivel has to take the despairing lunges of your fish. Use the best that you can buy and give them a close scrutiny before tying them into the trace. Types A and C are suit-

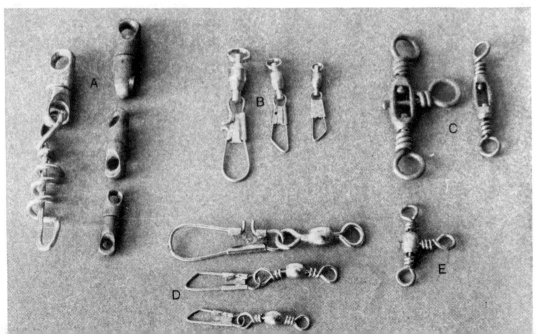

able with the larger sizes of patterns D and E. Those swivels that incorporate a snap link are very handy as they enable changing a trace without cutting the knot.

Leads

There are a multitude of shapes to pick from. I prefer the pyramid lead which should have wire loops at both ends. This is an important factor, for two joined leads of 10 ounces will hold the ground better than one of 20 as the first lead tends to anchor the second. It is a good thing to remember that if any particular lead will not hold, one of double the weight will not be too much to use. Casting bombs can be used for boat fishing; the problem with them is that they tend to roll around in current very easily. The pyramid lead has sharp edges which dig into the bottom. The casting grip lead will not hold in the bottom when fishing from a boat. It is intended to lie on its side with a very slight line angle. Boat fishing is an up-and-down affair.

Bits and pieces

A great number of boat fishing rigs are running legers of one kind or another. To work properly the lead has to slide easily along the line as the fish takes and moves off with the bait. Ideally it should feel little or no resistance to its run. There are several ways in which this can be achieved. Clements and Kilmore Booms or a simple lead link are designed to slide effectively and allow immediate

A blonde ray from the broken ground off Moyteague Point, Achill Island, Co. Mayo.

changes of lead size. Later in this chapter I will deal with their uses applied to specific rigs.

For generations booms of another kind were used to make up sea angling rigs. These were made in brass and were used to ensure that the bait stood away from the main line of the trace. In most cases they only succeeded in overcomplicating the tackle. I can see a number of uses today, but generally they are best avoided. Whiting have a nasty habit of taking a paternostered bait and then becoming hopelessly twisted up in the terminal tackle. Stand-off booms will help, in this instance, to avoid this. In conditions of slack tide booms will help in presentation of the bait.

I will discuss feathers at this stage, but only where they can be regarded as a method of catching bait. This artificial lure is formed by binding a couple of white or coloured chicken feathers on to the top of the hook shank. Fished paternoster style, strings of three, five or even twelve feathers are lowered into the water and vigorously jigged up and down. They simulate the fry of small fishes and will be grabbed by mackerel and other bait fish. It can only be regarded as a method of fishing for bait, as the mackerel are given no chance to display their speed and fighting qualities.

Baits for boat fishing
Certainly the best bait must be freshly caught mackerel. Naturally it is not always available. Mackerel rarely reach

Ted Tuckerman caught this red gurnard from a deep-water mark off the Blasket Islands.

our shores before early June and they are gone again by the end of October. They can be gathered and placed into deep freeze but have the unfortunate habit of going soft and mushy when thawed. Herring is another good bait. Like mackerel, it is full of oil and attracts fish by scent as well as by sight. Both of these fish can be fished as a whole bait, for tope, shark and other large fish. For the smaller species, a lash (fig. 7) or even strips of the fish (fig. 8) will make attractive hook-baits. The picture sequence shows how to cut a herring into lashes and strips for the hook.

Sprats, small pollock and coalfish are also useful bait, as are immature flatfish that have been taken on your bait. There is an Order prohibiting the keeping of immature fish of a number of species,

Three fish that are sometimes difficult to identify. The tub gurnard Trigla hirundo *(top), the grey gurnard* Trigla gurnardus *(centre), and (bottom) a red gurnard* Trigla culculus.

but they can be used as bait if taken by the rod-and-line angler.

Lugworm. A first-class bait for members of the cod family, some flatfish and a host of small species. They are available at most seaside tackle dealers but can be expensive. This is particularly so in the winter when low tide falls in the hours of darkness when professional bait diggers cannot see to dig. You can dig your own in many places around Britain. Look for a beach composed of a mixture of mud and sand. If lugworm are present they will indicate their position by little mounds of sand and mud often shaped like a coiled rope. Quite close to each mound there will be a small depression with a hole going down into the sand. I like to dig a trench in the sand about four feet long. Then I progressively dig backwards a spit at a time, working along the length of the trench. It is handy if two of you can gather bait together. One digs and the other angler searches the loose sand, turning it over to find the worms.

If you are going to fish almost immediately the worms can be kept in a bait bucket or plastic box. Keep separately any worms that have been cut into halves. Bleeding worms seem to kill the rest. If you are saving them for a future fishing trip, lay them out on a clean piece of newspaper so that they do not touch one another. In this way they will keep in winter for several days. In summer, or in times of stormy weather, lugworms are difficult to keep.

Ragworm. Another good bait, especi-

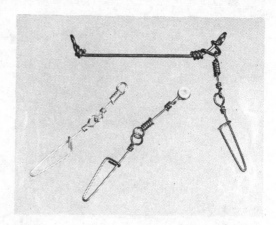

A Clements boom (top), *lead link* (left) *and a Kilmore boom. Any of these can be used to attach leads to a running leger.*

The skipper feathering for bait.

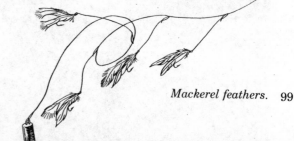

Mackerel feathers. 99

ally for bass and flatfish. The ragworm looks rather like an overgrown centipede with powerful nippers. These protrude from the head and can inflict a sharp bite. They come in a wide range of colours and sizes. The larger worm, deep red-brown in colour is often called a 'King rag' and can be broken up into pieces to provide a number of baits. These and the smaller pink and white ragworm are usually found close to the low-water mark in mud. Search the harbour and among rock and mud patches for these worms.

Ragworms are a good bait to fish on a two-hook tackle for bass in estuaries. The bait is run back downtide to where the fish are lurking. Quite often bass will chop the worm in half without taking the hook, and the double hook tackle increases the possibility of hooking a shy-biting fish.

A Mediterranean fish, the grouper.

Squid. Here is a bait that takes fish well but is becoming increasingly difficult to buy. It is used cut into strips and seems to attract fish by its colour and supple movement in the current. This is one of the sea angler's baits that can be simulated by an artificial lure. Plastic squids are available which will catch fish, especially when fished by the sink and draw method.

Shellfish. Most shellfish species will take fish, although their use is confined to certain areas of the British Isles. The sea anglers of the North of England use mussels, often in the form of a 'cocktail' bait in association with lugworms. The scallop is a killing bait in the western areas of Scotland. Cockles and whelks will·also be found on the hooks of sea

A porbeagle from a mark off the Isle of Wight.

Fig. 7 ▼

1. *To cut a lash from the side of a herring, make a cut into the fish and down to the backbone at the point shown.*

2. *Turn the blade of the knife and cut progressively towards the tail, keeping the blade as close to the backbone as possible.*

3. *Fold the fillet over and remove it from the fish.*

Fig. 8 ▼

4. *Each side fillet will make a number of herring strips. Try to cut the lash diagonally to make the strips long.*

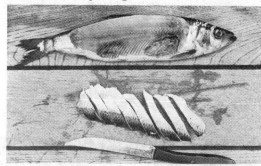

5. *Eight useful sized strips, a further eight from the other side and one fillet from above the backbone. There is a lot of bait on a herring!*

6. *To bait the hook, take the strip and place it on to the point at the darker and thicker end of the bait.*

101

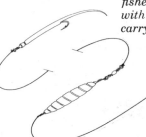

Fig. 9 *A rubber eel, fished on a long trace with a spiral lead to carry the bait to the fish.*

Fig. 10 *A pollack feather, tied to a 6/0 long-shanked hook and baited with a mackerel strip.*

A squid.

anglers in this area. Razor fish are a bass fisher's delight, providing they can keep them for bait and not eat them! Another first-rate hook offering is the clam, though they are becoming hard to find.

Artificial baits in rubber or plastic. These lures are constructed more to attract with movement than accuracy of representation. Consequently they are of little value to the lazy angler. They have to be *worked,* for the movement is imparted partly by the action of the current upon the body of the bait but mostly by the angler lifting and lowering them in the water. To be successful this type of bait should move as though it is a live fish because it has no smell or taste. None of these baits has any weight, so they will need a sinker to enable the lure to reach the fish (fig. 9). Rubber eels can be fished on a paternoster rig or below the lead.

A useful artificial bait for sink and draw fishing, the plastic prawn. It can be used with effect when fishing over sand near to reefs that hold bass and pollack. The success of this kind of lure depends on the way it is worked.

A variety of pirks. These are metal lures that are proving popular among cod fishers and other sea anglers who haunt the reefs and holding ground.

Jack Shell, with an East Coast codling.

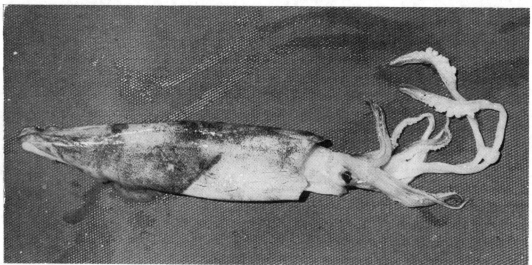

102

Artificial lures in metal. Unlike the metal spoons used by the shore fisher these baits have considerable weight. Some are up to a pound or more and they are fished on the sink and draw principle. Constant movement of the rod up and down is necessary to make the bait look like a small fish that is either wounded or frantically trying to escape from larger fish. Lures of the kind seen in the photograph have been particularly successful fishing over broken ground for cod. Catches of several hundredweights have been taken on metal jiggers or pirks.

Artificial lures in feather. These are different from mackerel feathers in that they are either bigger as in the case of the pollack feather (fig. 10) or are fished with the addition of a strip of fish bait.

The razorfish, a bait for bass anglers.

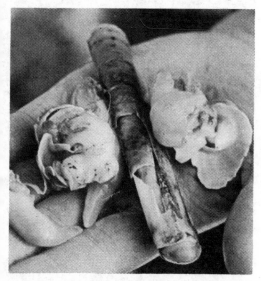

A good catch of fish, all members of the cod family.

Chapter 12
Boat fishing: situations and methods

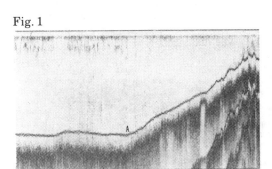

Fig. 1

Enough to bring a smile to the face, a fine turbot.

THE example that I will use exists off the coast of Essex. There are, though, many areas similar in underwater topography around Britain. The echo-sounder trace (fig. 1) gives some idea of the bottom, although in rather a condensed form. The trace shows the sea bed going out from the shoreline to a point two miles east of St. Osyth. The sounder was switched to give a wide range reading 0-60 feet, and it will be seen that the sea bed descends gradually to a depth of 30 feet. The small peaks at the right-hand side of the trace indicate a few clumps of uneven ground just offshore. This is the sort of ground over which it is possible to catch large numbers of cod in winter. The fish are not resident there, neither are they confined to a particular area.

At point A there is a shallow gully probably formed by the scouring action of strong tide. This gully has a shell bottom and appears to gather a concentration of fish midway between high and low water. Natural feed is swept into this spot on the strong flood and later, as the tide slackens, the fish move into the area to feed. With this kind of ground I expect to go looking for fish. Rarely does one expect them to come to the bait, except when a rubby dubby trail has been laid on the sea bed. The normal pattern of fishing is to steam out to point A, then the boat is allowed to drift until contact with the fish is made. If they come fast to the bait the anchor is dropped and a prayer is said that the boat is stationed over a route along which the fish are swimming.

As the anchor is lowered a half-gallon tin, with a series of holes punched in the sides, is tied on to the rope about six feet from the hook. This tin is filled with a mixture of pulped herring or mackerel, some bran and fish oil. The rubby dubby streams away downtide and will attract fish to the hook-baits, or least that is the theory!

When the tide is running strongly, leger rigs are used. They present a better bait to the fish as it washes around in current. When the tide goes slack a paternoster rig is made up to cope with the straight up-and-down fishing associated with this phase of the tide.

Whiting come along at this stage in the fishing session. They swim off the bottom and can be taken two at a time on the paternostered worms or fish strip. Due to the mud and sand mixture and the fairly strong currents from the local rivers, the water is highly coloured. To increase the chance of the baits being seen a spoon is often attached to the rig which will flutter in the current (fig. 2). Generally, artificial lures such as pirks and feathers do not work well in these conditions. This is possibly because the fish get a momentary glimpse of the baits as they pass through. I much prefer to have a bait which has smell.

Cod and whiting are the mainstay of our winter fishing. In summer small rays and tope, together with smooth hounds and other dogfish, arrive. The flatfish, plaice and flounders, can be caught and

Fig. 2 *An easily made cod spoon!*

Thornback ray Raja clavata

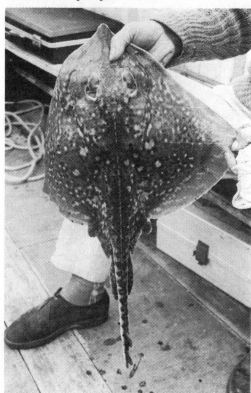

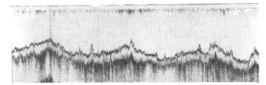

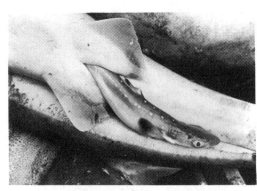

bass move up from the South into our estuaries and along the beaches.

Wind can be a nuisance on the east coast. There are few harbours so many sea anglers launch dinghies from the beaches. An east wind will put the fish off the feed. If it blows much above force three the sea piles up and the boats are kept ashore. Any wind blowing from nor'-west round to south is regarded as a suitable fishing wind for the small boats of East Anglia.

Fishing over broken ground

A vastly different proposition from the previous situation. This type of habitat holds fish. They both live and feed over broken ground and the variety of species increases. Pollack, coalfish and other larger members of the cod family seek this habitat. If the water is deep, then skate and conger eels will undoubtedly also be there. The sounder trace (fig. 3) was made off the west coast of Ireland in twenty fathoms of water. Our boat was steaming quite slowly, so an accurate idea was gained of what the sea bed looks like. Some of the peaks on the chart indicate that the ground is extremely broken. There are a number of large outcrops of rock mixed with the boulder-strewn bottom.

This kind of bottom can be fished both on the drift or at anchor. Drifting seems to be more profitable, but one must expect to lose leads and rigs in the rocks.

Drifting allows the use of much smaller weights because the boat is drifting over the ground at the same speed as the cur-

rent. A hard wind blowing in the same direction as the current will push the boat faster and a wind against the tide flow will slow the boat up a trifle. Nevertheless, drifting is a little easier than fishing to anchor, particularly as the boat presents her beam across the line of drift. This gives each angler more space from which to fish and at the same time keeps the lines separate.

Rigs can be either leger or paternoster in style, or a combination rig can be fished (fig. 4). It takes time to learn how to keep your lead out of the rocks. The best idea for newcomers is to lower the rig, touch bottom, then reel in a couple of turns of the handle. Occasionally drop the lead down to touch bottom again to be sure that you are fishing at the right depth. Don't allow the line to run off the reel if you think that you have lost contact with the ground. This will only result in forming a tremendous belly cf line over which you have no control and little chance of contact with your bait should you get a bite. The best system is to reel in, inspect the bait, and lower your rig again.

Fishing to anchor means that the boat's bow is pointing uptide, presenting the narrowest part of the hull to the flow. Naturally the stern is also narrow, but all the fishermen in the boat will have to fish over it. Whether you are legering or fishing a paternoster, there will have to be discipline in the craft. Supposing four anglers are aboard, the two inside rods should fish a lighter weight than the other two men. This will keep the leads

Fig. 3

Birth of a spur dogfish. The young of many of the shark family are born fully formed and ready to compete for available food.

106

and tackles apart on the sea bed. The current will force you all to use heavier leads to hold bottom than when drifting because the press of tide is pushing against the terminal tackle and against the amount of line that is run out. You would think that fine monofilament nylon would present little surface area to tide, but it does.

If your lead goes foul in the rocks it has to be broken out and that means hauling away, taking up the stretch, until a knot parts or the lead breaks free. On the other hand, if a lead becomes stuck in the bottom when drifting you should hold on hard and the drifting boat will pull the tackle free as she moves along.

Never allow the rod to touch the gunwale of the boat, either when pulling a fouled tackle free or when playing a big fish. If the rod is pulled across the gunwale it will probably break. Try to break the line—after all it is cheaper to replace the line than the rod! One other thing, be extremely careful when pulling on the line with your hands. Line under tension can give a nasty gash. Always wrap the line in a towel or around a piece of wood before attempting to break free.

So many species can be caught from this kind of ground that it is hard to suggest methods or bait. Ask the skipper what you can expect. Check whether fish will be bottom or midwater swimming varieties and tackle accordingly. Use a wire trace for those species with sharp teeth or rough skins.

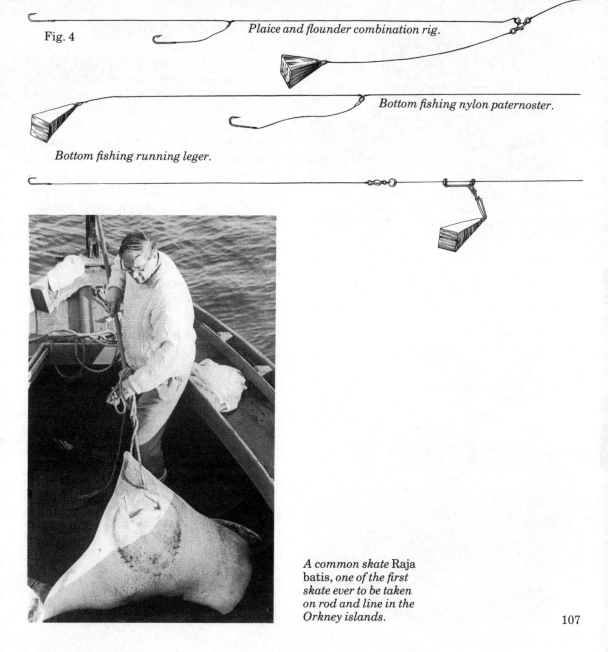

Fig. 4

Plaice and flounder combination rig.

Bottom fishing nylon paternoster.

Bottom fishing running leger.

A common skate Raja batis, *one of the first skate ever to be taken on rod and line in the Orkney islands.*

107

Bob Page, Secretary of the National Federation of Sea Anglers, inspects a small hake Merluccius merluccius.

The reason for a strong wire trace! These jaws can grind through the strongest nylon rigs. The wired link need only to be about a foot in length, joined to a forged steel hook.

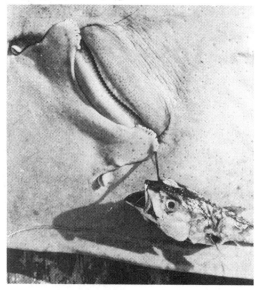

Angling over reefs and pinnacle rocks

It is very rarely that a boat can be anchored over this fishing habitat. The skipper will not want to lose his anchor or sea conditions may well prevent anchoring. Often an underwater reef will cause the current below the surface to force its way up, showing as a boil or overfall on the surface. The normal pattern of fishing is to go downtide of the reef or pinnacle and drift up to it. After passing over the ground the boat then returns to its starting position to drift once more.

Obviously the angler must be constantly alert to the changes in depth. Sometimes the skipper can give adequate warning of the rise in the bottom by keeping an echo sounder running. It is all a matter of reeling in the line but keeping the bait near to the face of the rock, working the bait to where the fish are. You will lose tackle, of course you'll lose it, but it is only by fishing tight into the rock that you will contact the really big specimens. Lower the gear, touch the bottom and then recover a little line. Not too much as the reef fish live in crevices and holes on the face of the pinnacle. They come out to grab a bait and plunge down back to their homes. If you can halt the initial lunge and so get the fish away from the reef the battle is more than half over. One species, the conger eel, elects to live among the rocks, so you will have to fish right in amongst them.

Don't attempt to fish for this species when the current is fast-flowing. They are

The largest of the British flat fishes, the halibut Hippoglossus hippoglossus.

relatively slow to take a bait – they mouth it and pull it about before swallowing. Slack water is the time to fish for these sinewy monsters. Both the conger and the ling will require wired traces and it is good practice to attach the lead on a rotten bottom. This is a piece of nylon of lower breaking strain than the main line. Should the lead go foul it is then possible to break it off without losing the fish or the terminal tackle.

Smaller fish, red bream, black bream, wrasse, pollack and cod, live over this ground. They will require a smaller hook and bait but so often you find it is the big fish that grabs the offering and smashes the gear. Reef fishing is a compromise between tackle strong enough to hold the big fellow and bait sufficiently small to attract the other species.

Artificial lures can be used over the reefs and pinnacle rocks. Fished *sink and draw* they will take most species that feed on live smaller fry. Pirks, which are heavy, and rubber eels, which need a lead to get them down, are taking over from natural baits with anglers that fish the reefs. It is all action fishing because the fisherman has to work the bait, continuously dropping it to the bottom, lifting the rod tip and lowering it. This movement causes the bait to rise in the water, then flutter down like a dying fish — a most attractive action; but fishing this method can be extremely tiring to the angler. An alternative is to place small strips of fish bait on to the hooks of a set of fairly large feathers. Cod, pollack and coalfish will grab these lures eagerly. Especially so when there is a strong movement in the water making the feathers stream out like a shoal of small fry! Last year, fishing a rock mark off the coast of Kerry in Ireland, I witnessed the catching of many good pollack on artificial lures. The angler, Ted Tuckerman of Torquay, never stopped working his baits for a second.

Wreck fishing

There is another kind of pinnacle, the wreck. It is not long after a ship goes to

the bottom before it attracts a population of fish. The bulk of the sunken vessel diverts the underwater current and creates a situation where small fish are able to live without being swept away. Weed becomes attached to the hull and this in turn encourages the growth of shellfish of many species. Big fish realise that the wreck gives them a vantage point from which to ambush the smaller residents. Soon they move into the top of the wreck. Gradually the tide will form a deep scour around the base of the hull into which conger eels will come. The sand and mud which has been scoured away builds up as a series of banks around the scour. Nature has created a new habitat.

Many vessels went to the bottom

A hard-fighting fish that comes regularly to our southern shores each year. It breeds on rough ground off Littlehampton. The black bream can give tremendous sport on light tackle.

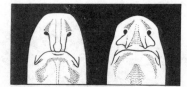

Identify the dogfish by their nasal flaps (left). The lesser-spotted Scyliorhinus caniculus. (Right) The bull huss or greater spotted dogfish Scyliorhinus stellaris.

109

around these islands, and although the authorities blow up the shallow-water wrecks, because they are a hazard to navigation, the deep-water hulks are allowed to rest in peace. Fishermen, particularly in the West of England, have lost much of their gear in these obstructions. With the arrival of the Decca navigating system trawlermen are able to plot the position of the wrecks accurately. They lost no more nets and they told other skippers just where the boats were lying. Soon sea anglers were paying visits to these well-stocked fishing grounds. Conger eels of huge size came to the gaff. Most species that were caught proved to be of above average size. These marks had never been fished with a rod and line and this was the only method by which they could be taken from the wrecks. There is a very rich food chain existing on a sunken vessel and this promotes the growth of huge specimens.

Wreck fishing is like angling over reefs and you will lose a lot of gear! Conger eels have a nasty habit of taking the bait and then diving into the hull or wrapping the line around the superstructure. It is heavy fishing that demands heavy tackle. A stout rod with at least 50 lbs. B/S line is required. Nylon is preferable, as braided line will easily fray on the metal of the wreck. Tides can be strong, which means a pound of lead or more. It is best to fish a single hook to a wire trace.

The skipper will try to anchor the boat in a way that will keep the baits dropping into the scour at the side of the wreck.

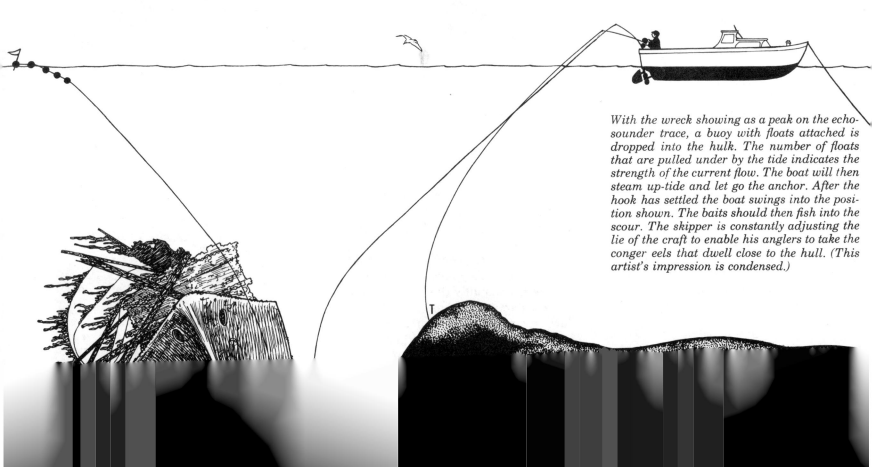

With the wreck showing as a peak on the echo-sounder trace, a buoy with floats attached is dropped into the hulk. The number of floats that are pulled under by the tide indicates the strength of the current flow. The boat will then steam up-tide and let go the anchor. After the hook has settled the boat swings into the position shown. The baits should then fish into the scour. The skipper is constantly adjusting the lie of the craft to enable his anglers to take the conger eels that dwell close to the hull. (This artist's impression is condensed.)

When a bite is felt wait for a steady pull, strike hard and do your best to get the eel up and away from the wreck. The conger will, in turn, do its best to get back from whence it came. If you get the fish out into clear water a steady pumping action will bring it to the boat. Keep the eel on a tight line; any slack and it will twist itself free of the hook and dive back to the depths. They should be gaffed into the boat and great care taken to keep them away from the feet of other anglers. A big conger can bite a man's hand off, so it is not wise to try to extract the hook from it's jaw until it has been killed. A hard blow across the vent of a conger will normally subdue, but rarely kill, the fish. Better you should fish a quick release trace attached to a link swivel. This can be taken off the reel line and the fish put into a fish basket or into the fish hold. Traces can be recovered later in safety.

Ling, pollack, cod, bream, tope can all be taken from a wreck by fishing over the top or slightly to the sides of the vessel. Indeed, when the tide is changing the angling boat will swing away off the wreck and the baits will come to rest on the piled-up sand rather than in the

This must be the largest catch of conger eels ever taken from one wreck, 2,862 lbs. in a period of five hours' fishing by six rods! Added to this catch were a vast number of cod, ling, pollack and other good pan-fish. The eels all went to the fish market where the largest weighed over 70 lbs., with many others going over 60 lbs. The wreck fishing out of Torbay is becoming famous throughout Europe and rod fishermen travel far for a 'Wrecking' session.

111

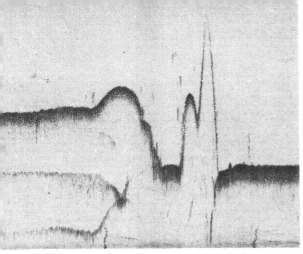

Echo trace from a wreck in shallow water.

Two specimen pollack and a fat cod from a wreck.

112

scour. It is here that turbot are to be caught. They live on these banks, rather like the open-water sandbanks, feeding on the small fish that are hustled around in the strong current eddies. Fish the same end tackle as for the conger because the eels often venture on to the sand and will cut clean through a nylon leger rig.

The offshore sandbank

Hear talk of a sandbank and you think of turbot. Sandbanks are formed by strong currents sweeping the sea bed, gouging gullies and piling up the mud and sand as banks. They are constantly changing in area and shape. So much so, that certain areas have navigational buoys that are moved constantly to keep pace with the formation of new dangers to shipping. The banks are normally in reasonably shallow water. Places, for example, like the English Channel where the Straits of Dover constrict the movement of the mass of tide. Sandbanks are inhabited by sand-eels and all manner of minute forms of life. They live in the sand but are washed out by the tidal action. The fish know this, so station themselves downtide of the strongest current force. This usually means that they lie over the hump of the bank awaiting the food that will be swept to them.

Turbot are fish feeders, they have enormous mouths and can move at speed over a short distance. If we anchor in such a position, uptide of the bank, that our legered baits will sink down on to the highest point of the sand it is then pos-

sible to trundle them back to the fish. This is best done by slightly raising the rod tip whilst at the same time letting a small amount of line flow from the spool until contact with the bottom is made (fig. 5).

In this way our baits can be made to cover the bank top to the gully at its base. Gradually a change in the tide will swing the boat to give a different downtide line. As the tide changes, from ebb to flood or vice-versa, the anchor is pulled and the boat moved to the other side of the bank.

Now to the end tackle. It is said by long-liners and sea anglers alike that turbot swim in pairs. This may or may not be true, but it is certainly worth baiting your rig with two or three strips of fish (fig. 6). This multiple-bait rig will also cover more bottom area and so increase your chances. Make up the tackle

How about this then? A ling Molva molva.

in nylon line; the turbot will not bite through it. The turbot is a soft-biting fish that will take time inspecting and mouthing the fish strip. Wire traces are too stiff and would tend to prevent the bait waving about in a natural fashion. If you feel a gentle plucking transmitted to the rod tip give it time to develop. When it results in a strong pull strike hard and pump the fish gently. The turbot itself doesn't give much of a fight but it will use the strength of the tide against you.

In the summer, tope and dogfish will often lurk in the gullies around these banks. Being predators, they wait to grab any luckless fish that is unable to combat the powerful currents. Fish a wire trace, leger fashion, with either lashes or a whole fish as bait. Mackerel, herring or sprats will serve to catch them. If you think that a tope is likely to appear, leave the reel out of gear but with the check on. Let the fish make its first run; it will then stop to turn the bait to swallow it. Flip the reel into gear and strike hard to set the hook as it goes off on a second run. For tope, have the wire at least four feet long

Fine fish at the gaff, a ling and a conger eel.

Haddock Gadus aeglifinus

Fig. 6 *Three-hook running leger rig.*

Fig. 5
The sandbank situation.

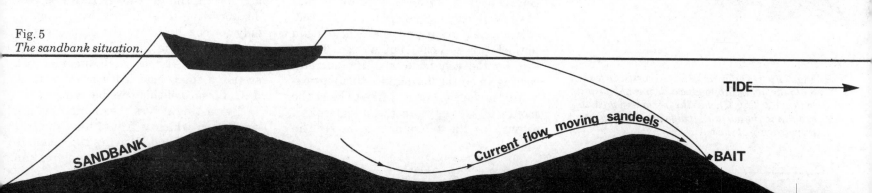

TIDE →

Current flow moving sandeels

SANDBANK

BAIT

One of the tastiest fish at table, a turbot, comes up from the sandbank.

Fish strip bait for turbot.

Fig. 7 *Fish-finder rig. A bored cork is threaded on to the hook link to give a degree of buoyancy to the bait. This washes the worm or fish-strip around in the current; it also prevents crabs from tearing at the bait.*

Bored cork

to avoid a line breakage through abrasion on the incredibly tough hide of this fish. The lead can be attached with a Clements or Kilmore Boom to allow it to slide freely along the reel line as the fish moves off.

In the wintertime cod frequent the banks, though rarely over the top where the currents are strongest. You will find them in the slack water downtide of the highest points. A fish-finder rig is useful as it will cover both the bottom and above-ground swimming fish (fig. 7).

Dinghy fishing in an estuary

I particularly mention fishing from a dinghy as this is one form of fishing that not only appeals to me but requires a small boat to cover all the potential angling spots.

It is frequently light fishing. An ultra-light boat rod or heavy spinning rod would be the correct choice, with a 10 lb. line on whatever reel you like best and leads of 1-4 ounces. In the winter I fish for codling which average 3 lbs. in weight. There are also flounders, dabs and a sprinkling of whiting and small pouting. Bait is usually lugworm, but I sometimes have deep-frozen mackerel to lure the cod.

Generally we expect sea fish to swim uptide; this is usual out at sea. In an estuary the fish swim with the current, coming in on the flood and returning seawards as the ebb starts. I like to be at the mouth of a river or in the middle of an estuary as the tide starts to flood. The

The British record cuckoo ray Raja naevus, *a fish of 5 lbs. Neil McLean caught this fish in Lamlash Bay, Isle of Arran, Scotland.*

best marks are usually close to the fairway, the deep channel along which the larger vessels proceed. I say close to, and not in, the fairway as it can be very disconcerting to be fishing away happily, only to look up to see the bluff bow of a coaster chugging towards you. Also the wash from even a small steamer can swamp a small boat if it passes too close to it. Beware of this possible danger.

By casting across the channel with a small lead which will just take the bait to the bottom and allowing the tackle to swing round in the tide, a large area can

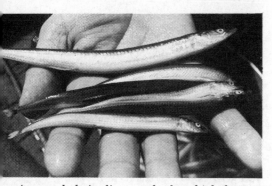

A superb bait, live sand-eels which have to be kept alive in a bait tank or courge.

be covered with the bait. A leger rig with the lead running directly on the reel line will suffice. If there are flounders about, attach a spoon to the hook link about four inches above the bait. It will flutter around stirring up little streams of mud that these flatfish will come to investigate. When the tide slackens change to a paternoster rig with the hook snoods about two feet up from the lead. This will take the whiting and pouting.

In the summertime the fishing of my estuary changes radically. The quarry is the bass. The estuary faces due east and has at its mouth a sandbar formed by the silt washed down the river over centuries. At dead low water this bar is almost visible and presents an obstacle to the movement of tide in or out of the river. Most anglers choose to fish the bar as the tide is dropping and the pressure of water from the river is at its greatest. The flow over the bar is indicated by a flurry of surf just beyond where the sand actually is. The dinghy is anchored in the river about fifty yards up from the bar. A rag-worm is placed on the hook, and the rig, a leger with a light lead, is dropped down in the current. It is then worked back through the boil of surf over the sandbar. Any bass present will be searching along the line of white water for food washed down by the river flow.

When they bite they hit hard and on the light tackle can put up a fantastic performance. Everything is on their side, the force of the current and shallow water that can give them room to manoeuvre. The light lead does not tether the fish by its head. It runs hard and has to be played right out before one can think of drawing it through the rough water and towards the landing net. The fishing doesn't last long, for as soon as there is a couple of feet of water over the bar the fish disappear. The surf line goes and the river mouth becomes full of sailing dinghies.

Higher up into the river, where there are a number of muddy creeks and the water spreads out to cover the saltings, mullet can be taken. I leave them to the shore fishermen and their patience. The arrival of the dinghy, motor noise and the associated disturbance of the water send the mullet scurrying away across the mudflats. Even when rowing the boat it is difficult to stalk the diatom feeders as they browse the tidal margins.

A small flatfish, the dab Limanda limanda, *easily identified by the curve of the lateral line over the pectoral fins. Sandy brown in colour, the skin feels rough when rubbed from tail to head.*

A sturdy dory for the inshore fisherman. The Yachting World *bass boat can be built from plans, by the angler or as a club project.*

Pouting Gadus luscus

115

Chapter 13
Beach fishing:

AS there are so many shorefishing situations and widely varying angling methods in use around the coast of Britain, I shall deal with places and tackles that have been successful for me. The different examples of angling mark do exist and will be identified in the photographs used.

Fishing the shingle beach

For me, and a great number of Southern anglers, this will mean winter cod that begin to arrive offshore late in October. The boat fishers, going out to distant marks, are first to catch these fish. Gradually as the temperature of the water cools the fish begin to come closer in to the shingle and the feed which exists there. Offshore they have been feeding on sprats and herring and reaping a rich harvest from the shoals. As these shoals disperse, the cod find their food harder to come by and a change in diet is forced upon them.

The shingle beach is so often a steep-to beach, with deep water close in to the anglers' feet. Cod will not swim into a foot of water as one would find on the gradient of a storm beach. This fish likes a fairly strong tidal movement which will scour amounts of feed from the sand and muddy bottom that exists beyond the shingle.

In the picture, which is of Dungeness, you will see that there is a strong surge onto the shingle. The tide is about half-way up on the flood and at this stage the fish are to be found at about ninety yards from the shore. Obviously this calls for a good cast, so the rods that are used here are strong and powerful poles that are capable of sending a lead out over a hundred yards. Not all shingle beaches require such prodigious casting, however. At Shingle Street on the Suffolk coast a cast of forty to fifty yards will put you among fish. Anglers are often responsible for driving feeding cod out into deeper

Beachcasting in sequence. With the angler's back to the direction of his cast and feet in the position shown (black on an imaginary line) he begins to swivel at his hips and on the balls of the feet. The build up of speed in the action is shown by the swelling arrow. The lead is released as the rod straightens and its flight followed with the rod tip.

Direction of cast

water. Picture the scene at Dungeness when some hundreds of fishermen are all hurling leads at the horizon. This must have a scaring effect on fish and they appear to move farther out to escape the noise as so many leads hit the surface and plummet down into the sea.

Because of the strong current and an equally strong surface surge, your rod should be one that will cast from 4 to 6 ounces and be strong enough to place the bait at distances of up to a hundred yards and land a heavy fish.

There are many such rods with a wide variety of actions. Reversed taper enables a rod to build up the compression slowly, unrolling and springing the lead away. Fast tapered rods have the power for heavy casting and playing of the fish, and are heavily built low down in the rod but with a steep tapered tip that shoots the lead away at the moment of release. The choice is yours; I prefer a rod that comes somewhere between the two in action, fairly fast taper for both casting and striking home the hook to a fish.

Most beachcasting rods can be used with either a fixed-spool or multiplying reel. For close-in fishing the fixed spool will perform its task adequately; longer casting with heavy leads is better done with a multiplier but is probably more difficult for the beginner to control. Practice, before you attempt to go fishing with a multiplying reel, is vitally important. The illustration (fig. 1) shows the typical shorefishing multiplier. As the cast is

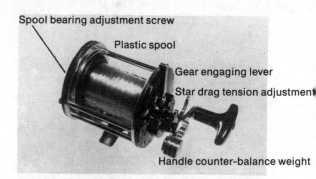

Fig. 1 *A wide-spooled beachcasting multiplier.*

Fig. 2

Fig. 3 *There are a number of different types of rod-rest. A tube, into which the rod butt fits, or a tripod which can hold more than one rod.*

Correct spool loading on a casting multiplier.

Fig. 4 *A tricky surge on a shingle beach. The angler's hand-gaff ensures landing the cod.*

about to be made the gear engaging lever is released, allowing the plastic spool to turn freely. The cast is made (fig. 2) and as the line runs off the spool the spool is thumbed to prevent the build-up of coils of nylon which could result in a 'bird's nest'! The reason for this happening is that at the beginning of the cast the reel spool begins to turn and accelerates at a tremendous speed to run off the nylon. As the lead begins to slow in its flight seaward the nylon itself does not, as it peels off the spool. If allowed to, the spool will continue to revolve at almost maximum revolutions, so a braking effect is required. This comes from the angler's thumb which should progressively slow the spool down during the latter stages of the cast. The gear lever is engaged, as the lead settles, and slack line is taken up. When cod fishing, the rod can be held or placed in a rest (fig. 3). Most fish hook themselves but will give you an unmistakable indication of their presence by a violent tapping at the rod tip from small fish, or a slamming over of the rod as a heavy specimen takes the bait. Pick up the rod, strike hard to ensure a positive hook-hold and play the fish in by pumping the rod up to a vertical position and recovering line on the downward stroke. This movement will take away undue pressure from the plastic spool as the nylon is recovered. Try to lay the line evenly across the spool with your thumb as you retrieve the line and bring in the fish. An evenly laid line will ensure that the next cast is smooth and trouble-free.

A word about the fixed-spool reel: if you do use it for casting heavy end tackle it is often a sound practice to place a rubber finger stool over the index finger of your right hand. Lift up the nylon on to the first section of the finger, open the bail arm and make the cast. You will find a powerful strain is placed upon the finger controlling the line and the protection gained by using the rubber stool is worthwhile.

Both the multiplying and fixed-spool reels should be loaded with nylon line. Depending on the weight of lead, size of fish and the nature of the bottom, a line of between 15 and 25 lbs. B/S would be right. Both reel lines can be fitted with casting leaders of heavier nylon joined with a double-blood knot to absorb the initial shock of casting heavy leads. Make them up to give you sufficient length to allow three or four turns on the reel spool plus the length of the rod and a drop of three feet. They also serve another purpose—when you have a big fish almost at the water's edge and there may be a strong wave action, tremendous strain is placed on the line. Waves will wash in a beaten fish but they will also wash the fish out again on the back-surge. It is sometimes necessary to beach the fish by waiting for a wave to lift it on to the shingle and then holding hard, preventing the fish sliding back. As soon as it is still move quickly, grab the fish or casting leader and haul your cod up into safety. A small hand-gaff (fig. 4) can help when landing fish under these conditions.

There are two basic terminal rigs for this form of sea angling, the nylon paternoster and the running leger. I think the paternoster is the best for cod fishing as the fish is not tackle shy. It will pick up the bait and swallow it, then move on looking for the next morsel. In conditions of clear water and slack tides, the fish may get a clearer look at the bait and tackle. It may then be advisable to use a running leger, which allows the fish to pick up the bait and move off without feeling a great resistance to its movement. The nylon paternoster (fig. 5) is formed from a piece of line, *the same breaking strain as the casting leader,* about four feet long. Make a loop at the half-way mark using a double-blood loop (fig. 6) and attach the hook by either cutting one side of the nylon or by slipping the loop through the eye of the hook and over the shank. If tied on, a tucked half-blood knot will hold best. Alternatively the hooks can be tied to short droppers, which are in turn attached to the blood loop. Don't overcomplicate the rig or use metal booms or spreaders. They will only cut down your casting distance and tend to tangle the tackle on the sea bed. Tie a link swivel to the bottom of the paternoster, it makes lead changing so much easier. The rig is then joined to the reel line which has a link swivel tied to the end of the leader.

The shape of a lead for good distance casting is important. It is necessary that the bulk of the lead is in a correct forward position (fig. 7) so that it will fly true and

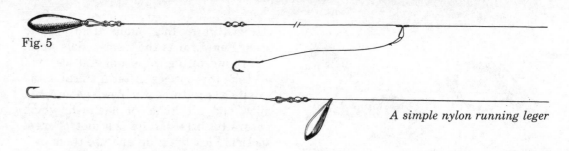

Fig. 5

A simple nylon running leger

will not tumble through the air setting up resistance to its flight. Where there is a strong lateral current along the beach it is necessary to use a grip lead with wires that dig into the sand and prevent the lead from rolling round. A grip lead will keep the bait where you want it and on a crowded beach will help to prevent tangling other anglers' lines, always a problem but one that can be minimised. After casting let the lead settle, then pull it slowly until you feel it catch in the bottom then tighten the line.

In the hook selection shown in chapter 10, the irons E, F, G and H are suitable for shore-fishing. Sizes will depend upon the amount and type of bait in use, together with the species being sought. Look at the point of the hook regularly because frequent retrieval over shingle can soon remove a sharp point from any hook. Snap-link barrel swivels are most used for trace and lead attachment (see Chapter 11). Give them a steady pull before using the trace to make certain that they are up to the job. Sizes 5-10 are suitable for the reel lines quoted.

It is difficult to name the best baits for cod, there are so many and this fish

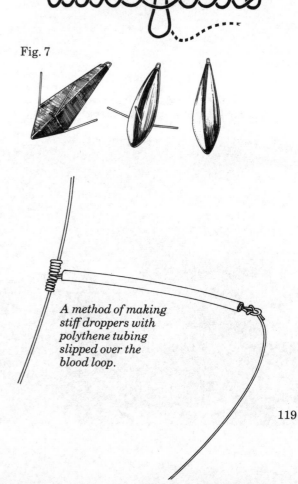

Fig. 6

Fig. 7

A method of making stiff droppers with polythene tubing slipped over the blood loop.

119

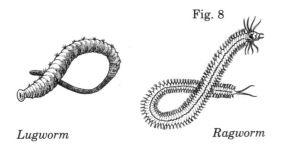

Fig. 8

Lugworm   Ragworm

Only water between the author and America.
Casting to the bass in the breakers.

changes its feeding habits from area to area. Lugworm is the most widely used, but ragworm (fig. 8), squid and fish will all take this species. After a storm many small sea creatures are blown ashore, sea mice and all kinds of shellfish which naturally form part of the diet of most species. Pick them up and use them as a hook-bait. A few minutes will gather enough to fish a tide and the bait is free!

Fishing the storm beach

If you have such a beach close to your home you are probably a bass fisher. Most of our storm beaches face south-west into the teeth of the big ocean swells which produce the surf on the shore that brings the bass and a sprinkling of flatfish species. The bass is a strong-swimming agile fish that seems to enjoy the breakers crashing over its back. It roams to-and-fro along the length of the curling wave searching for sand-eels and worms that have been driven out from the sand. Along a length of strand, with three or four creaming breakers running onto the sand, you feel part of the fishing that you are doing. You cast to a position behind the third or, if you can manage it, the fourth wave and let the bait settle. Then it is a waiting game; bass will not be spread along the entire length of the beach. They will be working the surf, moving from spot to spot. With luck they will arrive at your hook offering. If you get a fish and then have a quiet period move to one side or the other of your fishing position, for it is found that the angler can keep with the fish as they feed and move along the surf-line.

Surf-fishing is a roving sport and the rod must always be held in the hands. A bass does not always announce its arrival with a thumping knock to the end tackle; too often it can take the bait from the hook without the angler being ware of it. There are so many types of bass bite. The slackline take where the reel line falls flat in the water because the fish has run in towards the angler's feet is one example. The only way to hit this bite is to run back out of the water and up the beach until you can feel the fish, then strike and play it. It is not possible to reel in the slack line quick enough to re-establish contact. Sometimes bass, and particularly big fish, will give slight trembling knocks just perceptible by holding the reel line between the fingers. Opinions differ as to how this bite should be handled. Some anglers say that the bite should be allowed to develop into something more positive. I prefer to strike at the slightest indication of an offer!

Occasionally a tweaking pull to the bait is from a small flatfish; only experience will tell you what is attempting to take the bait. Flounders are often found on a bass strand, especially when there is an amount of fresh water running into the sea from a stream or small river. Once hooked you will know whether the fish is a bass or otherwise, as very few fish can fight like a bass in the surf.

After a swell has died away the surf will dwindle to a mere pattern of small waves. It is then that other species such as tope, monkfish and small rays will put in an appearance.

When fishing for bass and the smaller fish, tackle can be a good deal lighter than would have been used on the shingle beach. A 10-12 feet rod, easy in its action and casting leads of 2-4 ounces is my choice. A small diameter multiplier or fixed-spool reel, loaded with 14 lbs. line double-blood knotted to a 18 lbs. B/S casting leader is just right. Either paternoster or running leger terminal tackle can be used. I would choose the running leger rig (fig. 9) as it can be used with both casting bombs and grip leads. Tied in this form the lead will not tangle the trace and result in losing the value of a freely

Fishing the wild surf of a storm beach.
A released bass moves off to sea.

121

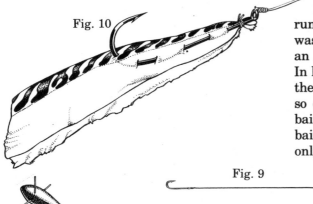

Fig. 10

Fig. 9

running leger. With this rig the bait washes around in the current presenting an attractive offering to shy feeding fish. In heavy surf, where the fish will not see the component parts of the tackle quite so clearly and the surf is pounding the bait around, fish tend to snatch at the bait. This is probably because they get only a quick glimpse of it, pick it up and press on. Then the nylon paternoster is as good a rig as any.

Bigger species can be taken from a storm beach and therefore the tackle will have to be strengthened. The rod used for winter codding is admirable with a reel carrying line of 20-25 lbs. and plenty of it. A minimum of 200 yards is necessary for fish that run.

A monkfish Squatina squatina

Leslie Moncrieff, night fishing at Stradbally on the Dingle Peninsula, beaches a spurdog.

When tope or other predators with sharp teeth are expected, use the normal running leger, replacing the nylon with a wire trace. Ensure that the lead link runs smoothly on the reel line as these fish have to be given time to move off, stop to turn the bait and then swallow it. If they feel any resistance to their efforts to make off with the bait they will probably drop it. Fish baits, mackerel, herring or fillets of flatfish are good baits. Try to cast them with an easy swinging action so as not to throw the bait off the hook; alternatively you can tie the bait on to the trace with elasticated thread (fig. 10).

The sandy bay

I have in mind a quiet little bay, bordered on both sides by cliffs that fall sharply into the sea and at the head a steep incline of grass and heather. At the base of this slope, down which there is a path giving access, is a broad ribbon of white sand. From the water's edge the bay shelves gently into forty feet of water within sixty yards of the sand. Beyond, it deepens rapidly to sixteen fathoms at the mouth of the bay. Along the sides, under the cliffs, the ground is rough with small boulders that have fallen over the years, providing a haven for small pollack and wrasse. In the centre of the bay the bottom is dotted with patches of weed with the occasional outcrop of rock.

Sand-eels live in the bay along with worms and some shellfish which have attached themselves to the rocks. There are two ways in which to fish this spot.

Codling and a flounder from the shingle beach.

Denis Burgess fishing for cod in Yorkshire.

A 'Chicken' turbot from the sandy bay.

With a light beachcaster such as the bass rod from the sand, or float fishing from the cliffs at either side of the bay.

What can we expect to catch? Over the sand there are dabs, fine, fat, fleshy dabs, many going over a pound. When the tide is flooding the sand-eels come out of the bottom and draw turbot into the bay—not huge turbot but fish of 4-6 lbs. that really go on the tackle in use. A couple of ounces of lead, a running leger rig with a single 1/0 long-shanked hook and it is all go!

For the turbot I fish a mackerel strip (fig. 11) which will sway in the current simulating live eels. The bite is hard to describe; you feel a gentle sucking pull which may continue for some minutes. The pull must not be struck, for the fish is only mouthing the mackerel strip. Then gradually the rod tip is pulled round as the fish moves; it is then that a sharp strike is called for. It is often said that the turbot does not fight. Don't you believe it,

A large sandy bay 20 miles deep—Luce Bay.

for in shallow water this species can certainly move. Not a screaming run—rather a positive move-off that pulls the tip over in a series of erratic thumps as the fish uses its strong tail to swim in the undulating fashion of these flats.

Dabs take the lugworm best of all; the baits hardly hit the water before a fish is interested. The bite is a sharp tap-tap on the line accompanied by fierce tugs transmitted to the rod tip. Strike immediately and the fish is yours.

Unlike the turbot and dabs which can bury themselves in the sand to escape predators, the pollack and wrasse seek the security of the rocks and thick clumps of underwater weed. They do venture out on to the sand alongside the cliffs, but seldom go far. The easiest way, and by no means unpleasant method, to catch them is to float fish. As the water is quite deep a sliding flat technique has to be adopted. The rig for this will be dealt with in

greater detail in Chapter 14. Bait for the two species that inhabit the cliff face is easy to come by. Limpets are prised from the rocks by sliding a knife under the shell edge and used as the hook-bait. They are first-rate for wrasse, as this fish spends a great deal of its life tearing the same limpets from the rocks with powerful jaws and teeth. Pollack will take them, although mussels collected at low water are probably better. The flatfish baits, lugworm and mackerel strip will also lure wrasse and pollack.

The sandy bay shown in the photograph is in the north-western corner of Ireland. Had it been in the south-western area this bay would certainly have produced bass. Many small crabs are found in the rocks at low water, so these, in the soft and peeler stages, would make a fine hook-bait for bass.

Crab

Fig. 11
Mackerel strip

*Spinning from the shore
at Salcombe in Devon.*

125

Chapter 14
Shore fishing

THIS type of fishing environment presents a number of serious problems. Let me analyse the different permutations of situations that can be met:

Fishing from rocks out on to a sandy bottom.

Fishing from rocks into a rocky bottom.

Fishing from rocks into a mixture of rocks and thick weed.

The first category is reasonably easy to cope with from a fishing point of view. One can either fish the bottom using a paternoster or leger terminal tackle, though in shallow water of twenty feet or so float fishing is better when the fish are living close-in under the rocks. Strong tide makes float fishing difficult at times but the method is worth pursuing when the fish are swimming in mid-water, particularly along the face of a rock ledge.

Fishing from Filey Brig, a mark in Yorkshire.

The prime consideration should be for personal safety. When fish are coming to the rod it is very easy to forget that tides rise and cover some rocky ledges. Spray can make weed-covered rocks slippery and most unsafe when the angler is wearing rubber boots. Before fishing from any rock station ensure that one has a line of retreat in the event that the tide rises farther or faster than was thought.

The second situation is more difficult, one that I have experienced to my cost. I went to Yorkshire to try the autumn cod fishing from a number of shore marks between Flamborough Head and Filey Brig. Naturally, I took my normal cod fishing gear, a 4-6 ounce rod equipped with a medium-weight multiplying reel. My companions, great cod fishermen, were carrying heavy 12 feet hollow glass rods with huge Scarborough centre-pin reels loaded with extremely strong nylon. To me, their gear appeared outrageously strong for the small codling I had been

Fishing for wrasse from the rocks at Doonbeg on the Atlantic coast of Ireland.

led to expect. But when we arrived at the first fishing place I began to get an inkling of what to expect. We cast from uneven slippery rocks out into a rock-strewn bottom. I waited for a bite, got one, struck and found that the lead was fast in the rough ground. Result, one lost fish and a new trace to tie. As time went by I lost trace after trace. The line was not strong enough and the multiplying reel could not retrieve the lead fast enough to make it rise from the ground clear of the jumble of rock in its path. On the other hand, my companions were getting bites and with the fast retrieve rate of their reels lifting fish and end tackles clear of obstructions to the path of the tackle. I cut down the amount of

Tough fishing country, the kelp jungles of the Yorkshire coast demand a special kind of tackle and highly developed local techniques.

The harbour at Tarbet, Argyllshire.

127

terminal gear lost by tying the lead on to a length of rotten bottom, nylon of lower breaking strain than the main trace. This allowed the lead to break off whilst still leaving the trace and hooks free to come back to me. I think that a good practice when regularly fishing this ground would be to collect old nuts and bolts and pieces of useless metal to act as sinkers. Those I would not mind losing!

I would still choose to fish this rocky habitat, because it is here among the tangles of kelp and boulder-strewn bottom that the fish are to be found.

The last type of ground is undoubtedly the worst. But from my point of view the best fishing is here among the rocks and kelps. The Scarborough fisherman's gear is absolutely correct for the environment. For he can hook a fish and raise it quickly from the bottom avoiding the rock, then with the strength in the line and rod draw the fish through the weed to his gaff. Tackle, in these circumstances, is not balanced to fish. It has to be suitable for the conditions that one finds.

Angling in the estuary

River mouths provide many types of angling and species of fish, from spinning for bass to legering a mackerel lash to catch tope, and the lightest form of sea angling, float fishing with freshwater tackle for mullet. The movement of the tide will play a much more important role, bringing fish within casting range and stirring up the mud and silt to encourage the fish to feed.

An ideal spot for mullet and bass among the weeds.

Most of our saltwater species will move in with the flood tide. When the effect of fresh water is at its least they will search the ground and then depart as the ebb tide begins. Some species, like mullet and flounders, that are tolerant of a high freshwater content in the estuary, will stay. Fish for the flounders with a leger rig (Chapter 12, fig. 9) using lug or ragworm on a small long-shanked hook. Roll the rig round in the current by casting across the stream and allowing the end tackle to sweep around. Just enough lead to hold the bait on the bottom is needed, for the value of this technique is that it will cover a great deal of the bottom searching out dormant fish.

Mullet fishing is another case for carrying the bait to the fish rather than expecting them to come to you. Mullet are extremely shy creatures and easily frightened. When they are in shallow water feeding over mudflats or along the sea-walls, their dorsal fins are seen jutting out of the water, which makes finding the shoal quite easy. They can be confused with shoaling bass, but the illustration *(right)* should clearly indicate the basic difference between these species. Tackle up your coarse fishing leger rod with the reel you use to trot a river. Five pounds line is just strong enough to fish with whilst remaining fine enough to avoid scaring off the mullet. They have good eyesight—they need it to feed as they do on minute marine organisms. Choose a small but strong hook and ensure that the point is as sharp as you

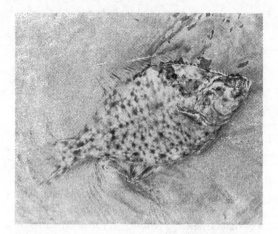

This little fellow is the flounder Pleuronectes flesus. *When released from the hook the fish will often dig itself into the sand to hide. It also steals baits intended for bass and larger species of coastal fish.*

can make it. Pinch on a morsel of breadpaste and trot the tackle downtide to the mullet. If you are lucky you might hook one, but they are notoriously difficult to catch; if it happens play the fish gently. It is a strong species but has a rather soft mouth that easily tears.

Fishing from piers and in harbours

Here is the opportunity to fish in reasonably deep water without having to set foot in a boat. There aren't many species that cannot be taken at some part of the year or other from these fishing platforms. Even shark have been seen lurking around piers on the south coast of England during the past couple of years. Tackle is strong and, as with rock fishing, has to be because it is the place and way in which an angler is forced to fish that dictates his tackle strength. As there is a little more room per angler than in a boat, rods can be longer—7-8

Bass Dicenthracus labrax

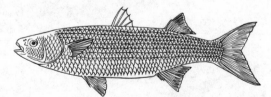

Thin-lipped grey mullet Mugil ramada.

feet is a fair length. The conventional shore-fishing rod is too long to be handled and cast with from a pier. Choose a rod that will give the most satisfaction in playing the fish, but remember it may have to lift the fish vertically a considerable height.

Multiplying or centre-pin reels will perform their function well; they should have metal spools to avoid crushing under the pressure of tightly wound nylon. Very little casting is strictly necessary; the bait can be lowered and then dropped down the tide, covering a lot of ground as it travels. Obviously the lead must be only just heavy enough to hold bottom to do this. Both leger and paternoster rigs can be used to fish these stations, depending on the species sought: leger rigs for bottom feeding species and paternoster tackle for mid-water swimming fish. When fishing inside a harbour where there is little current to speak of, it is useful to attach the hook snoods to the paternoster rig with stiff wire booms. These will stand the hooks away from the trace and prevent tangling.

Spinning for saltwater species

If you are an angler who likes to cover ground with constant activity take up spinning. It is truly light tackle fishing, for the tackle can be balanced to the weight of the fish with just enough allowance made to cope with the strength of tide.

Three fish can be said to be spinning species: inshore pollack, smaller than the specimens found in deep water over wrecks and reefs (a couple of pounds would be an average size); bass of all sizes, as this is strictly a coastal species; and lastly mackerel. I use two different rods for sea spinning. One of 8½ feet in hollow glass with a spigot ferrule, which is normally used with a fixed-spool reel and 8 lbs. line. The other rod is longer and more powerful and I find that a line of 12 lbs. gives me the right balance. The former light sea spinner is very useful spinning from a dinghy where it also doubles as an ultra-light bottom rod for

Spinning from a rock ledge. These ledges can be treacherous when wet, and it is wise to make certain of your foothold before fishing.

the small flatfish and sea breams. The ten-footer has the steel to cope with large pollack and bass from the rocks; its main advantage is that being longer I am able to control a fish more positively. The rod will resist the deep plunges made by pollack that will grab the spinner and go down hard into the kelp.

Look to the fittings on a sea spinning rod; salt water can be cruel to inferior chrome rings and winch fittings. Always clean the reel and rod with fresh water after fishing to remove the salt. The same attention should also be paid to your sea-spinning lures. Treble hooks should be of stainless steel or similar material that will not rust.

Two major groups of artificial baits can be had for saltwater spinning: lures, made in rubber or plastic, that represent a sand-eel or other small fish (fig. 1); then we have a fantastic number of metal lures, some with a pretence of repre-

A nice catch of fish taken at night.

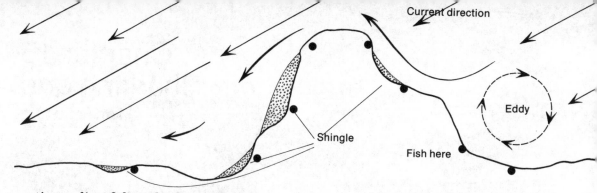

senting a live fish and others that look like nothing on earth (fig. 2). The secret of both groups is that they wiggle, wobble, duck and dive or troll in a way that imparts life in their movement through the water. Action in the bait is the important thing, colour and shape are secondary considerations. Lures vary in weight; some require the addition of a lead to enable them to be cast or fished at depth. I prefer to have sufficient weight in the lure itself. Any lead which is fixed on the line ahead of the lure will have a dampening effect upon the action of the lure and make it return up the line during the cast.

Fishing for mackerel is often just a bait-catching process—a string of feathers taken down into the water by a heavy lead. But mackerel fished for on a spinning rod with a small trout spinner can provide terrific sport. The mackerel, a member of the tunny family, is fast. Use your light gear and I am certain it is a fish that will provide you with a thrill. Garfish, often found swimming among mackerel shoals, are also capable of tremendous speed and acrobatic performances on the surface of the sea.

Tidal action on a headland. The current flow will tend to carve the rock away, forming little shingle and sand beaches where the slack-water eddies are situated.

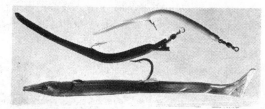

Fig. 1 *Three rubber eels for spinning, 'sink and draw' fishing and trolling. (Top-bottom): Red-gill eel has superb action and appearance. A black rubber eel, it works well in clear-water conditions. A white eel made from polythene tubing.*

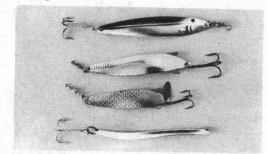

Fig. 2 *Four of my favourite spinning lures, all will take bass and pollack. The top three simulate the appearance of a small fish. The other is a 'German Sprat' and can be worked like an eel.* 131

Chapter 15
Sharking and holidays

Shark are strong fish and can be of great weight. A groin pad and kidney harness will allow the angler to use his tackle and strength to subdue the fish.

STRANGE to say, fishing for shark is rarely undertaken by the average sea angler. There are two kinds of shark fishermen. There is the expert who will travel hundreds of miles and devote many hours to the capture of these huge fish. Also the holiday angler who maybe sees a billboard on the quayside in the West Country and goes gaily off to tangle with these fish.

Serious shark fishing is not for the faint-hearted; considerable physical exertion is needed in many ways. The shark can be a porbeagle or mako, weighing hundreds of pounds, or just a small blue shark. Shark angling, as it is practised in this country, entails drifting a boat for long distances and in all weather conditions. It is quite easy to become exhausted by simply standing up. The motion of the boat and continued effort to keep one's balance can be immensely tiring.

On the other hand, the blue shark has become a tourist's fish. During the peak holiday months in the West of England large numbers of these fish arrive off the coasts of Devon and Cornwall. In times of fair weather and calm seas boatmen advertise shark angling trips for the blues. All the gear necessary to catch a shark is provided in the boat within the price for the day's angling. Because the boatman does not want his tackle lost or broken it is often far too heavy for the size of fish that one expects to find. Over the last few years the average size for blue sharks taken has been 40 lbs. Yet

Held securely, with a rope around the body, this fish had the hook removed and was released to fight another day.

the tackle is a stout almost unbendable rod, with lines up to 130 lbs. B/S on huge reels. Small wonder that the blue shark has gained a reputation for not fighting. With this gear it cannot fight and the catching process has been reduced to just hooking and winding the poor beast into the boat.

Using light tackle, related to both the fish's size and ability, the blue shark can and will produce a good fight. A rod, balanced to 50 lbs. B/S line, such as one would use for tope and conger will handle the big blues. Some shark anglers would prefer even to scale down to 30 lbs. class line and an all-action rod. The only part of the tackle that has to be heavy is the trace to prevent the fish biting through the hook link or rubbing through the reel line. A trace made up to the size and pattern shown (fig. 1) would be quite capable of holding blues and porbeagle shark up to 250 lbs.

The hook, a forged iron about 8/0 in size, is attached to the mouthing piece using ferrules on the wire. The first length of trace needs to be of 250 lbs. cable-laid wire, bare or nylon-covered, joined to a quick-release heavy-duty swivel. This is joined either to a length of heavy long-liners nylon or another piece of wire to which is attached a further swivel. The reel line is joined to the shark trace using a Policansky knot, for it is usual and desirable that the reel be loaded with Terylene braided line.

The system operated among shark fishers is to seek fairly deep sea, away from the coloured coastal water. The boat is set on a drift and bags of rubby dubby are hung over the side. The rubby dubby is made from crushed mackerel or herring mixed with pilchard oil and bran. As the boat drifts a film or trail of oil is deposited on the surface of the sea. At the same time minute particles of fish

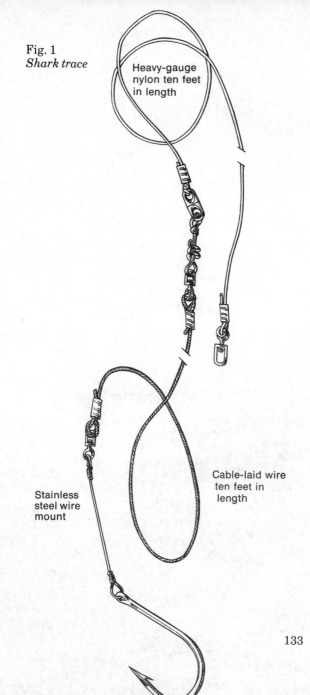

Fig. 1
Shark trace

Heavy-gauge nylon ten feet in length

Cable-laid wire ten feet in length

Stainless steel wire mount

and bran will sink in a steady stream down into the depths. As the boat is pushed along by the wind the rubby-dubby trail will increase in length. Any sharks coming upon either the surface oil or stream of fish pieces will follow to investigate the source.

The angling baits are drifted away from the boat, supported by a float. The float can be a partially-inflated balloon, a piece of buoyant material such as cork or expanded polystyrene block. It is important to set the baits at differing depths and distances from the boat. Supposing for example, there are four anglers fishing, two baits would be forty yards out, one at five fathoms and one at ten. The other baits could be at thirty yards distance and both set at fifteen fathoms. The risk of tangling the various traces is lessened, whilst the water is fished down in depth.

Sometimes shark are seen following the rubby-dubby trail on the surface, but more often the arrival of a fish is noticed as a vigorous bobbing of one of the floats. As the reels are in check but out of gear, the fish is able to take a bait without feeling any resistance to its run. At the same time the angler knows what is happening because the check on the reel will start to click. At this point the other men in the boat should retrieve their lines and baits. This will prevent tangled lines and the possibility of losing the fish should slack line develop as the tackles are sorted out.

The shark is allowed to make an unhindered run. It will then stop to turn and swallow the baitfish. As it moves off on a second run the reel should be flipped into gear and the rod held awaiting the tightening of the line. When this is felt the rod must be struck hard and positively, back over the shoulder to set the rather large hook. The fish will now be hooked in the mouth. If you delay the strike it is almost certain that the shark will have swallowed the bait down its throat or even into the stomach. If hooked deeply the fish will not put up a good performance and will probably have to be killed.

Let the shark run but keep a constant pressure on it. Adjustment of the star

A 70 lbs. blue shark is boated in a flurry of spray.

drag during the fight, so that even though it is taking line the fish is working hard against the drag, will subdue it more efficiently than dragging the fish on a tight line. When the runs slow down in the speed and distance that the fish goes, increase the drag and begin to pump the rod whilst recovering line on to the spool. You may find that a heavy fish will make a number of further runs during this time. Let it, because it is important that the fish should be quiet and played out when it is finally brought to the side of the boat.

When the trace is seen appearing above the water, one of your angling companions must take hold of the trace and draw the fish into gaffing or tailing distance. This is a dangerous time. Keep out of the way so that if the fish should decide to make one last desperate plunge all he does is to let the trace fly out over the gunwale. The angler holding the rod must be prepared for this to happen. It is good angling to slacken off the drag when the trace is being handled so that if a sudden run occurs the line will peel off the reel and not break.

If the fish is to be gaffed aboard, sink the head of the gaff into the water beyond the fish. With a firm upward stroke draw the point into the body behind the dorsal fin. Two people will probably be required to haul the fish up and over the side. Despatch the shark with a hard blow across the skull midway between the eyes. *Don't* leave it to thrash around in the well of the boat.

All four species of shark found in our seas can be fished for on the drift. Mako, thresher and blue sharks will be swimming in midwater as they feed on fish that swim in shoals in the upper layers of the sea. The porbeagle shark tends to live over reefs and other rocky ground where it feeds on fish that reside there. Recently there has been a move to fish for this species by a trolling method where the bait is pulled along behind while the boat steams over habitat known to hold this fish. The method has proved successful in Ireland and no doubt we shall see more anglers coming to this style of shark fishing. ▶

A stainless steel stiff wire mount, with two hooks, for a mackerel bait.

A porbeagle shark from the waters of the Isle of Wight. The area has developed as a shark fishery in recent years.

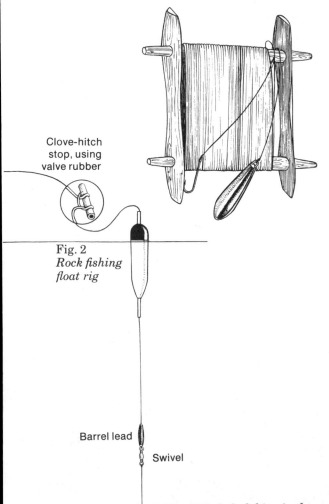

Clove-hitch
stop, using
valve rubber

Fig. 2
*Rock fishing
float rig*

Barrel lead

Swivel

*Two little lads fishing in the
harbour. These boys have
wise parents, for they have
equipped the children with
life-jackets. Harbours have
sheer walls, often without
ladders or steps, so a simple
precaution has been taken.*

Holiday fishing for the children

Parents often find themselves at a loss to amuse children by the seaside. Dad intends to fish but neither parent can justify buying sophisticated tackle for children who may well rapidly lose interest. The answer is a handline. This is a simple frame on which is wrapped a length of strong synthetic line with a couple of hooks and a lead to sink the whole caboodle to the bottom. Obviously a young child will not be able to cast, so the handline must be used where there is sufficient depth of water for fish to be.

The hooks, fairly small and about size 2, are baited and the line is unwound from the frame and lowered until the lead hits bottom. The frame can be jammed into a rock crevice or tied to a bollard on the harbour wall. This will prevent a large fish from pulling line and young angler into the water. The line is held between the fingers to detect a bite. As it is made from quite stout

material a fish can be hauled up from the water without fear of breakage.

Sooner or later, children want a rod. If you feel that they are interested enough in the sport to warrant buying tackle, invest in a solid glass rod with a simple fixed-spool reel. They can either fish the bottom using a paternoster rig or running leger (fig. 5, Chapter 13). This style of sea angling can very quickly bore children as there is very little to see. It is just a case of baiting and waiting!

Better they should learn to float fish. Here there is something to see and the chance of losing end tackle is considerably lessened. The rig (fig. 2) is simple to tie and costs little for materials. Bait can be worms, tiny strips of fish or shellfish pieces. Places suitable to fish from are harbour walls and flat ledges of rock into a reasonable depth of water. Depending on the time of year, mullet, wrasse, small pollack and flatfish could be amongst the youngster's catch.

A warning note . . . never let small children fish unattended. Apart from the obvious danger of falling into the water, all too easy when they get excited, there is always the possibility of hooking themselves. Everybody does this at some time. It is the only way in which to learn not to—but it is better that the experience should not come when a child is alone.

If you are the parent of adventurous children, the sort who have to try everything, don't forget to rig them out with an approved lifejacket or buoyancy aid.

Chapter 16
Seabirds and shorelife

Gannet Sula bassana

Fig. 1
Great black-backed gull
Larus marinus

Fig. 2
Lesser black-backed gull
Larus fuscus

SEA anglers have wonderful opportunities for studying the birds of the seaside and the ocean. Rarely does a fishing vessel return to the harbour without a flock of attendant gulls. During the summer months, when anglers are seeking the mackerel shoals to provide bait, gannets will pass over flying high, ever searching the sea below them. From a hundred feet or more they watch for the shoals of fish coming close to the surface. Having found them, the birds dive repeatedly to make their kills. The intelligent angler looks for this feeding activity. When the birds are *working* he knows that it is time to lower the feathers down to the fish and fill the bait box.

Birds of the ocean can be divided into two major types. Firstly, those that alight on the waves to pick up scraps of food and, secondly, those that dive below the surface to catch fish and other creatures.

One group of birds, the gulls, will also be found scavenging along the shoreline. They also travel far inland to be seen in fields, in parks and around the towns far from the sea. Gulls vary in size; the greater black-back has a wing span of about 36 inches, whereas the smallest of the gull family, the little gull, is a mere 17 inches across the wings.

The birds' body size, colour of plumage and the shape of the head are reliable identification features. It is possible to get quite close to many of our sea birds. I have found that inspection of a cliff nesting position from a boat just off-shore is tolerated, but a visitor arriving on foot along the cliff top will put the birds up from the nest. This, I think, is linked to their constant awareness of enemies. Nesting birds of any species expect predators to appear from the sky.

A pair of low-power binoculars greatly assists the bird watcher. A X30 magnification can be held when viewing from a boat. Any greater magnification is difficult to use when a boat is rocking on a swell.

Let us look at some of the head shapes and coloration of the more common European gulls. The greater black-back gull is most often seen in the north and west of the British Isles. It rarely nests inland, favouring a sea cliff or offshore island on which to breed. The head (fig. 1) is of a young bird clad in first-year plumage. This voracious killer has a formidable beak admirably suited to tearing small birds apart, which it does throughout its life. The adult gull has a rich black mantle with white underparts. The yellow bill has a red spot on the angular lower mandible.

A smaller version of this gull, the lesser black-back, is sometimes seen accompanying flocks of herring gulls. The adult bird's mantle is a dark slate grey and the legs are yellow. This gull (fig. 2) shares its larger cousin's taste for carrion. It also will steal eggs and chicks from the nests of neighbouring gulls in the breeding colony. Nesting in Scotland, Ireland and some parts of the north of England over the years, the gull

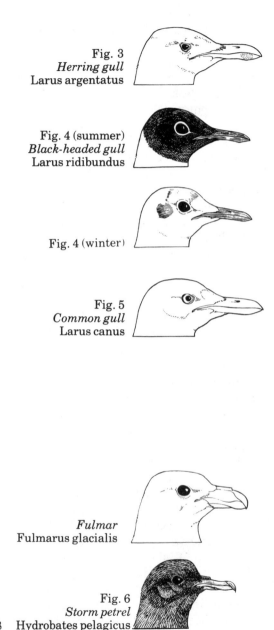

Fig. 3
Herring gull
Larus argentatus

Fig. 4 (summer)
Black-headed gull
Larus ridibundus

Fig. 4 (winter)

Fig. 5
Common gull
Larus canus

Fulmar
Fulmarus glacialis

Fig. 6
Storm petrel
Hydrobates pelagicus

has changed its way of life. During the winter the lesser black-back forsakes the sea and becomes a familiar sight scavenging, along with herring and black-headed gulls, on rubbish dumps.

The herring gull, with a less angular lower half to its beak, must rank as the commonest species of gull in this country. In former times it nested on the cliffs and coastal grasslands. Now it is to be found breeding on the roofs of seaside houses and even on inland lakes and moorland. Practically all forms of food will be readily eaten. The grey back, or mantle, is lighter than that of the lesser black-back and the herring gull has pink legs (fig. 3).

Most of us will have seen the black-headed gull following the farm tractor, seeking wireworms and other minute life thrown up by the ploughshare. Many of them live in the heart of our biggest towns and cities. As with the other gulls they are scavengers. They like to live close to man rather than braving the elements at the seaside during the harsh winter months. They can easily be wrongly identified. In winter this gull loses the dark brown-black hood and exhibits just a few brown blotches over the ears and around the eyes. I have often watched this pretty little gull feeding on flies over a reservoir. Very quick in its movements, it resembles a tern or swallow as it swoops and flutters to catch insects on the wing (fig. 4).

The common gull (fig. 5) is by no means common, although there are large breed-ing colonies in the North. It is found wintering with our other resident gulls, far inland, but will return to the coast to breed. It is a small gull with a delicate yellow beak which lacks any form of red spot. Its legs are a dirty grey-green, whilst the grey back is similar to the herring gull.

When fishing off the western coast of Scotland the boats are followed by a grey-backed sea bird. This bird, a fulmar, is not a gull but a member of the petrel family. Compare the head and beak with that of the gulls. It is entirely different, for it is a tube-nosed bird. The plumage is similar in colour to the herring gull but the fulmar is a sturdier, plumper bird. The flight is unique, a stiff-winged gliding low over the waves. Sometimes the wings almost touch the water as without effort the bird soars into the teeth of a stiff ocean breeze. At one time this species was rarely seen on the British mainland and was found only on the Outer Hebrides and St. Kilda. Now it comes regularly to breed, staying to raise only a single chick before departing to spend the winter far out over the ocean.

There is another little petrel that spends most of its life at sea, the stormy petrel (often called 'Mother Carey's Chicken') that follows transatlantic liners and other ocean vessels. It is a small sooty-brown bird (fig. 6), with a white rump and square-cut tail, that patters with its feet on the surface of the waves. Whilst apparently walking on the water

An immature kittiwake Rissa tridactyla

it feeds by dipping its head below the waves, feeding on small oily particles of fish offal, oil and plankton. Shark fishermen can expect to find this petrel following a rubby-dubby trail.

The stumpy, fat little birds that dive below the surface to feed or to escape the presence of a boat are auks. They are all powerful underwater swimmers that use their wings to propel them on the feeding foray. The black bird with a white breast and white slashes across an angular beak is the razorbill (fig. 7). It spends most of the year at sea but in the early spring returns to lay a single egg in a communal breeding site on sea cliffs or rocky shores. The razorbill will be found sharing the nesting site with another small auk, the guillemot. Though they are both black and white birds, the guillemot has a sharply pointed bill, so is easily recognizable. They arrive during January and February to begin the ritual of mating and nesting on the cliffs. Only one egg is laid and it is a wonderful sight to see the birds incubating their

eggs. They stand astride the egg, often in long rows on the cliff ledges with other rows below and above them. The birds look like guardsmen standing stiffly to attention. Here and there, amongst the auks, a solitary kittiwake adds a splash of startling white to the black ranks. During the winter, guillemots display large patches of white on their necks with a streak of vivid white back behind their eyes. Our illustration is of the bird in summer plumage (fig. 8).

Sea anglers who live in the far north, around the Shetland Isles, may see another auk. It is now a rare visitor to this country. The little auk (fig. 9) lives in the Arctic ocean areas, rarely leaving the pack-ice of Spitzbergen. Winter gales will often drive this bird to our shores along with other rare species like the king eider and ivory gull.

Surely everybody knows the last of our illustrated auks (fig. 10). The puffin nests in a number of places on the west coast of Britain and Ireland and is pictured on the Lundy Island stamps. Unlike the other auks that nest on a cliff face, the puffin digs a burrow in the soft turf at the top of the cliffs. Sometimes, if there are rabbits inhabiting the area, it will use a ready-made rabbit hole. A single egg is laid in May and, after hatching, the chick is fed by both parents. I have fished off the coast of Kerry with thousands of pairs of these lovely birds constantly passing overhead, carrying a number of tiny fish held sideways across their bills. Unfortunately, the puffin

Fig. 7
Razorbill Alca torda

Fig. 8
Guillemot Uria aalge

Fig. 9
Little auk
Plautus alle

Fig. 10
Puffin
Fratercula arctica

seems to be disappearing from former breeding colonies in the south of England, where once it nested in thousands.

Two more diving birds are seen regularly by sea fishermen, the cormorant and the shag. They are similar in appearance and size, though the cormorant has a distinctive white patch at the base of the throat. Both of them are dark in colour; brown-black in the case of the cormorant, and green-black feathers clothe the shag. During the breeding period the shag has a feathered crest on the head and prefers to live on the rugged cliffs of the coast. The cormorant is likely to be seen inland on reservoirs and lakes.

There are many sea ducks. Two of them are of interest to the anglers who fish either the rocky coastline or the mudflats or estuaries. The eider duck is the bird that gives us eiderdown. The lining of the nest is of soft downy feathers stripped from the breast of the duck. Man discovered the insulating properties of this down and now collects the feathers to warm his own nest! The drake is a handsome bird with a black cap, wings and underparts. The rest of the plumage is a brilliant white. The poor duck is dowdy by comparison. She has mottled brown feathers with black barring admirably suited to blending into the vegetation in which the nest is built. The incubation of the eggs is only undertaken by the duck and it is said that she does not eat or drink during the 28-30 days of sitting.

Shelduck
Tadorna
tadorna

Fig. 11
Oystercatcher Haematopus ostralegus

140

Cormorant Phalacrocorax carbo

Eider drake Somateria mollissima

Most species of duck have males displaying gorgeous feathering whilst their mates are dull. Our other sea duck, the shelduck, is unique in that both sexes are highly coloured. The male's red bill has a knob in front of the eyes to distinguish him from the duck. Both have black heads, a white breast with a chestnut band crossing it and white underparts. The wings are black and white. Because of the distinctive colouring of both sexes which would easily be seen by potential nest robbers, this bird seeks to hide the nest in holes or under dense cover.

Black and white seems to be a predominant coloration amongst our sea birds. It gives a remarkable degree of camouflage to their body shapes and they quickly become lost in the boulders and rocks of the shore. Here the sunlight casts a hard dazzling whiteness on the rocks, giving an inky blackness to the shadows. Sometimes it is only the call of a shorebird that gives it away. One call, a piercingly piping trill, is unmistakable. The oystercatcher moves busily over rocks uncovered by the ebb tide. It constantly pipes either to warn its mate of your presence or to establish territorial rights with other oystercatchers (fig. 11).

Take care when you walk the shoreline. Watch where you place your feet, as some birds nest in a mere scrape in the shingle. Don't stay too long at a nesting site in case your presence causes a bird to desert the eggs.

The rockpools

Unless we all take up aqualung diving or grow gills, much of the life in the sea will remain hidden from us. Techniques for the collection of underwater specimens can never replace seeing the animal living and feeding in natural surroundings.

Twice a day nature provides us with a window into the undersea world. On each phase of the tide, part of the littoral zone of the seashore is exposed to our gaze and exploring fingers. The ideal opportunity for close examination of marine animals that inhabit the tidal areas is provided on the rocky coast. Here little pools that are capable of supporting life are left by the receding tide.

The inshore area is divided into three sectors. A shallow zone always covered in water from the low-water mark outwards. An intertidal zone where tides rise and fall, replenishing the pools with water and oxygen. A splash zone where the waves rarely reach except at times of storms and exceptionally high tides.

Adults and children alike can have great fun exploring the wonders of the rockpools. Each puddle is an eco-system in its way. To learn about the animals that live in this situation it is advisable to provide yourself with a few simple tools: a fine-mesh net to catch the creatures in, plus a pocket lens, preferably with two or three glasses giving different magnifications. A pair of tweezers to pick up tiny specimens and some empty

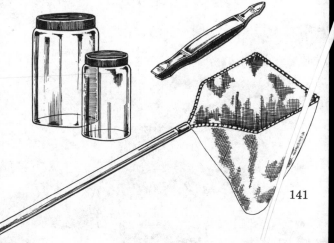

Keith Linsell

Life in the rockpool

1. Short-spined sea scorpion *Cottus scorpius*
2. Egg case of the lesser-spotted dogfish *Scyliorhinus caniculus*
3. Bladder wrack *Fucus vesiculosus*
4. Ringed plover *Charadrius hiaticula*
5. Common goby *Gobius minutus*
6. Slipper limpet *Crepidula fornicata*
7. Common limpet *Patella vulgata*
8. Acorn barnacle *Balanus balanoides*
9. Common mussel *Mytilus edulis*
10. Tube sea-squirt *Ciona intestinalis*
11. Common periwinkle *Littorina littorea*
12. Beadlet anemone *Actinia equina*
13. Breadcrumb sponge *Halichondria panicea*
14. Shore crab *Carcinus maenus*
15. Lugworm *Arenicola marina*
16. Lobster *Homarus vulgaris*
17. Chiton *Lepidochitona cinereus*
18. Hermit crab *Eupagurus bernhardus*
19. Common sunstar *Solaster papposus*
20. Common whelk *Buccinum undatum*

screw-top jars from the kitchen are also needed.

You would be most fortunate to find all the animals that are contained in this drawing of a rockpool by Keith Linsell. The area has been condensed and shows a representative sample of what might be found. The seaweed is bladderwrack, a common weed of the intertidal zone. It normally grows in the water but can exist out in the air provided the weed is occasionally wetted. It has an irregularly-shaped frond or leaf with a central raised spine along the length of each branch. Often there are pairs of inflated bladders set in the plant. When damp bladderwrack is olive-brown in colour. This dries to a brown-black when it is uprooted and blown above the tideline. Seeds are expelled into the water from oval, granular spore cases.

Seaweed, of all kinds, provides shelter for small animals as well as shade from the hot sun. Among the fronds, at the base of the plant, little shore crabs will hide from the fish that visit the pool

when covered by high water. They are our commonest crab, green in colour, rarely growing very large. As they grow their bodies become too big for the shell, so they split the shell open and emerge as a naked creature. It is at this time that they are vulnerable to being eaten. Shore fishermen gather the 'softies', as they are called, to use as a superb bass bait. Gradually the shell hardens and the crab emerges from the shelter of weeds and rocks to feed once again.

The hermit crab does not have the bother of splitting his shell and growing another. This crab remains naked throughout his life, protecting a soft body by backing into an empty whelk shell or other suitable home. When moving he carries his home with him and when it is too small to contain his bulk he finds a larger shell.

The awesome crustacean with the huge nippers and long antennae is a lobster. It can be found hiding amongst boulders in shallow water, but usually prefers to make its home farther offshore. On a fishmonger's slab it is a bright red, a colour induced by boiling. In the wild it is a brilliant blue.

Any amount of snail-like animals can be found in the pool. They are known as univalves as the shell is in one piece. These creatures are good to eat, whether by man or by fish. The whelk, common or edible periwinkle, common limpet and slipper limpet can all be used as bait for rock-dwelling fish, or cooked for the family. Another fine shellfish is the

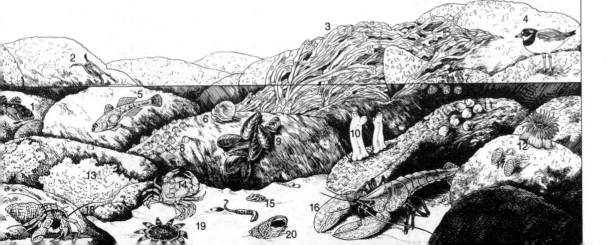

mussel, which is a bivalve having two hinged shells.

Barnacles are peculiar animals that fasten themselves to the rocks in great numbers. There are so many at times that the shore appears white when seen at a distance. As the tide flows, the acorn barnacle opens tiny plates in the top of the conical shell. Small finger-like appendages emerge to wave in the current seeking tiny morsels of food.

If you search the face of the rock closely you may find a tiny mollusc. Looking rather like a flattened, oval-shaped wood louse, if it is dislodged from the rock it will probably roll up into a ball. This animal is a chiton or 'Coat of Mail' shell.

The two animals looking like snowmen, but made of jelly and almost transparent, are sea-squirts. Widely varying in colour, this species of squirt can also be seen attached to the piles supporting piers and harbour walls.

The beadlet anemones, along with many other species of plant-like life, provide the vivid colours to our rockpool. With multi-tentacled bodies waving in the water, they are animals without a skeleton. When uncovered by water the tentacles are withdrawn into the body which then looks like a lump of stiff jelly. Do not remove them from the water because their wonderful shape and colour will disappear. Large areas of underwater rocks may be covered in a thick spongy growth, most often green but with varied patches of brown and yellow. It is another animal, the breadcrumb sponge, which

grows around the base of many of the seaweeds. A primitive form of life it feeds by sucking in water and extracting plankton and oxygen. The water is expelled via a duct that may be common to a number of animals attached to one another.

Two fish live their lives in a pool such as this, the common goby and the short-spined sea scorpion. The goby is hardly more than two inches long and brown-grey in colour with two rather large dorsal fins. If you can catch one, turn it on to its back and look at the underside of the body. Your magnifying glass will be handy here. Look at the space between the pectoral fins. In most fish there are two pelvic or ventral fins. In the goby family these have become fused together to form a sucker with which the fish can attach itself to a rock or some other hard surface. The purpose is relatively easy to understand. When the tide is flooding waves will cause quite a disturbance to the pool. Little animals and plants could be washed about and smashed among the rocks. Most creatures in the pool, therefore, have a means of fixing themselves to a solid object.

The short-spined sea scorpion is a frightening little beast, brightly coloured with sharp spines on the gill cases and first dorsal fin. The fish is small, rarely exceeding eight inches in length. Beautiful colours, red, brown and white, are spotted over a dark brown body. Be careful when handling this fish. The spines are not poisonous but can inflict

a nasty wound.

Out from our rockpool, over the sandy ground, a lesser-spotted dogfish attached its eggcases to the weed growth. The tide has washed the empty case, or 'Mermaid's Purse', into our pool. The rectangular, leathery wallet has tendrils at each of the four corners. These hold the purse fast to the weed during the time that the egg is developing into a miniature replica of its mother.

There are many species of starfish. They can have as many as twelve arms, though most species have fewer. Arms get broken off the animal and can grow again, though never to quite the same length or shape as the original appendage. The animal on the sand is a common sunstar. Red or purple hued, it has ten arms. The strength of starfish is phenomenal; they can open a closed mussel by forcing the shells apart to feed on the animal within.

This little pool has a sandy bottom. It is rare to find any depth of sand in any like situation as the tidal scouring would normally wash sand and debris away. Worms live in this sand, burrowing U-shaped tunnels with a blow hole at one end and a pile of sifted sand at the other. Lugworms are probably the sea angler's favourite bait and will catch most of the fish found inshore.

The splash zone has its inhabitants, marine insects such as bristle-tail flies and sea beetles which live and hide among the lichens that grow above the water-line. Occasionally we find a small, dainty-footed bird picking its way through the flotsam. A distinctive black collar across a white breast identifies it as a ringed plover. His mate is probably close at hand nesting on the pebbles beyond the high-water mark.

The inter-tidal zone is a fertile belt on the shoreline. Many creatures, often thousands of them, occupy any square yard of sand and shingle. I have mentioned just a few, so when fishing is poor take a closer look at the open-air laboratory nearby to see what you can find.

Chapter 17
Clothes and commonsense

SUMMER fishing presents few problems of dress to anglers. Most of them tend to keep their favourite old clothes to be worn on the day out. I must confess that I have a number of jackets, some getting very ragged and smelly, in which I feel very comfortable. They are part of the ritual of fishing.

For the summertime shower, a nylon anorak with overtrousers is the best wet-weather outfit. Light in weight, they pack into an extremely small space in the pocket or tackle bag. Coarse fishermen like to carry an umbrella. It gives ample protection when sitting on the fishing stool and at the same time will cut down strong wind. This is an important consideration when fishing from a static position. When you are immobile a wind across your back can be uncomfortable and unhealthy. The spinner or fly fisherman finds the wind more of a nuisance to his casting activity than to his personal comfort. Ensure that the anorak has draw strings or elasticated cuffs at the wrist to prevent water running back up your arms at the moment of casting. A simple hood will keep your head dry and many nylon anoraks have one tucked away under the collar. Always fit overtrousers outside gumboots so that water will run off rather than into your boots.

Wintry weather will bring the other problem of how to keep warm. It is absolutely pointless to wrap oneself up to a state where it is both difficult to cast or move quickly. Several warm but loose sweaters worn over a thick shirt with woven string underwear will keep you happy. Again the wind will play a role in chilling the angler. Either an anorak of close-woven nylon that is also waterproof or a quilted nylon jacket and trousers will keep the wind out. Most people find that the physical exertion required to get to their fishing is inclined to bring on overheating. After half an hour or so they then begin to feel chilly. I think the answer is to travel fairly lightly clothed. Carry a further sweater in the fishing bag, this can be put on after cooling off.

For many years we all wore outer clothing of heavy P.V.C. or oilskins. They certainly kept the wind and rain out but during the cold weather became very stiff. Modern proofed nylon suits do not stiffen nor do they crack in icy weather. Buy your suit slightly on the large size. This will allow you to wear additional sweaters and at the same time not inhibit your casting ability.

Sea anglers should never wear waders or heavy sea boots when boat fishing. Fall over the side and the waders will fill with water and act as two anchors, dragging you below the waves before help can be mustered. Wear rubber-soled shoes with canvas uppers in warm weather as these will clean up easily after a day's fishing. During the winter, short rubber boots are the answer. A couple of pairs of socks will keep your feet warm. Again buy them a size too large; if you fall in they can be kicked off.

There are several makes of fine padded and waterproofed suits on the market. Clean them with a mild detergent brushed over the outer surface and rinse off with fresh water. It will pay you to clean all the salt from your clothes as well as your tackle after a day on the boat.

On the occasions when somebody in the boat succumbs to sea sickness they will feel the cold much more than the other members of the party. A modern space blanket takes up little room in the tackle box and will prevent serious chilling of the unfortunate angler.

Sea sickness

Sea sickness is a curse to many people. Drugs are available from your chemist and if one brand does not work try another. If you are prone to sickness, take the recommended dose at least two hours before sailing. Always eat a good breakfast but avoid fatty meals — cereals with toast are best. Take warm drinks with you to sea and avoid excessive amounts of alcohol the night before.

There are two other hazards to health, and the effects of both are magnified when out at sea. Sunstroke is very dangerous and it is not always apparent at the time. Loose floppy hats will protect the top of the head and are doubly useful if they are large enough to cover the back of one's neck. Don't scorn suntan products in hot weather either.

Sunlight reflected from the water and gaily coloured paintwork on the boat will cause strain to the eyes. Sunglasses, especially with polarized lenses, will do two things. They will protect the eyes by cutting down glare and also enable the angler to see down into the water more clearly. This is particularly important to salmon and trout fishermen who often walk the river to spot fish in their lies before fishing to them.

Safety

I would not wish to dampen anyone's enthusiasm for winter fishing, but I feel one or two points should be stressed. In bad weather, and certainly when there is poor visibility or extreme cold, never fish alone. It is too easy to have a mishap which could prevent you from reaching help. Tell someone at home where you are going and when you expect to be back. This is absolutely essential for small-boat sea anglers. The coastguard is there to watch over the inshore boat. Ask his advice as to sea and wind conditions that can be expected during the trip. Then make it clearly understood to him where you intend going and your expected time of return. Carry the few aids to safety, a life-jacket for everybody that is aboard, hand flares, an anchor and sufficient rope, a bailer and spares plus essential tools to remedy minor faults that may arise with the engine.

Safety at sea and a regard for your own life and that of your companions is commonsense. There will always be another day to go fishing, so if things are not absolutely right go home and plan for the better day.

Chapter 18
Places to fish

THE maps, keys, species and regulations are intended to serve as a guide to enable the travelling angler to plan fishing visits. Quite obviously the list has been curtailed to enable me to cover the five countries forming the British Isles. Anglers seeking detailed information on specific areas should consult the publications named.

Contrary to general thinking, there are still a great number of places where fishing is free. Many waters that are controlled by clubs, hotels and large fishing associations have day permits so enabling the travelling angler to sample the fishing in distant waters.

England and Wales

There are 26 River Authorities covering the two countries. They issue licences to fish within the waters that they control. These licences can also be bought from tackle dealers, hotels and some post offices. The regulations concerning seasons, size limits and angling methods allowed vary from area to area, so local information should be sought before you plan your visit.

The national close seasons are as follows:

Salmon, November 1st-January 31st.
Trout (except rainbows), October 1st-last day of February.
Coarse fish, March 15th-June 15th (both days inclusive).

There may be special regulations prohibiting fishing for pike during the early part of the coarse fishing season. Also, some authorities ban the use of gaffs to land salmon during the late months of the salmon season.

Most licences have the sizes of takeable fish printed on the reverse sheet of the form. It is unlawful to keep fish smaller than the 'size limit', they must be returned to the water with the minimum of injury. For example, an immature salmon is one less than 12 inches long.

It must be understood that a river licence does not give an automatic right to fish. Permission, from the riparian owner, or a permit is also required.

A typical river board licence.

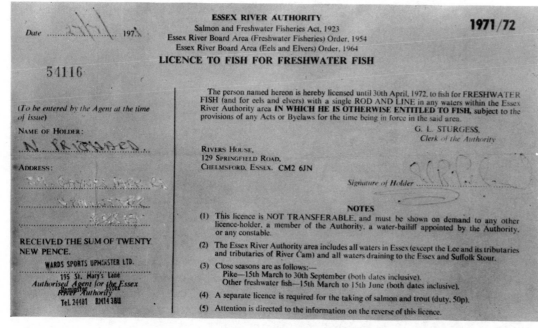

Key to specific sea areas

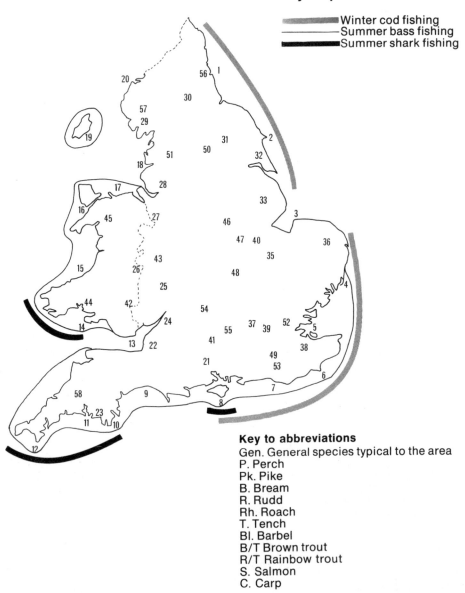

- ▬ Winter cod fishing
- — Summer bass fishing
- ▬ Summer shark fishing

Key to abbreviations
Gen. General species typical to the area
P. Perch
Pk. Pike
B. Bream
R. Rudd
Rh. Roach
T. Tench
Bl. Barbel
B/T Brown trout
R/T Rainbow trout
S. Salmon
C. Carp

Sea fishing areas

1. Northumberland coast. Good winter cod fishing.
2. Flamborough Head and Filey Brig. Good coalfish and cod.
3. Hunstanton and North Norfolk coast. Gen., tope and flats.
4. East Anglian coast. Cod in winter, bass and flats in summer.
5. Thames Estuary. Gen. from boat and shore.
6. Upper Channel. Gen. boat, cod and flats from shore.
7. South Coast, Newhaven to Little-hampton. Gen., from boats, black bream in summer.
8. Isle of Wight. Gen., bass and por-beagle shark.
9. Lyme Bay. Gen., mullet, bass and flats.
10. Torbay and wrecks. Gen., bass and conger.
11. Plymouth and Eddystone. Gen., bass and shark.
12. Cornwall. Gen., bass, mullet and shark.
13. Bristol Channel. Flats, bass and tope in summer.
14. Gower Peninsula. Bass, tope and shark.
15. Cardigan Bay. Gen., bass and tope.
16. Anglesey and Menai Straits. Gen., bass, tope and mullet in summer.
17. North Wales coast. Good shore fishing in summer, tope and skate.
18. Lancashire coast. Whiting and cod in winter, flats and skate in summer.
19. Isle of Man. Gen., pollack and flats.

20. Solway area. Gen., tope and flats in summer.

Coarse fishing areas

21. Hampshire Avon and Dorset Stour. Gen., Pk., Bl., and grayling.
22. King Sedgemoor and Huntspill Drains. B., P., Rh., T., C. and some trout.
23. Slapton Ley. Pk., R., P. from boats.
24. Bristol Avon. Gen. coarse with some trout.
25. Severn. Gen. coarse and game fish. Bl.
26. Rivers Wye and Lugg. Gen. coarse fish and game species. Chub and grayling.
27. Cheshire and Shropshire meres. Gen. coarse. Good canal fishing in the area.
28. Lancashire canals. Gen. coarse, many small streams and reservoirs.
29. Lake District. Pk., P.
30. Northern streams. Mostly trout but some coarse fish.
31. Yorkshire rivers. Gen. coarse fishing. Bl. and grayling.
32. Hornsea Mere. Famous for pike, P., Rh.
33. Lincolnshire rivers. Gen. coarse.
34. River Trent. Gen. coarse. Badly polluted in parts.
35. Great Ouse and tribs. Good coarse fishing, zander and pike.
36. Norfolk Broads. Gen. coarse fishing, good Pk.
37. Thames river system. Gen. coarse fishing. Best in winter after boat traffic ceases.
38. River Medway. Coarse fish with occasional trout.

39. London reservoirs. Rh., R., B., Pk. and P.
40. River Nene. Gen. coarse with carp in winter at Peterborough.

Game fishing areas

41. Hampshire Avon and area. S., B/T and sea trout.
42. River Usk. S., B/T.
43. River Severn. S., B/T and grayling.
44. S. Wales rivers. S., B/T and sea trout.
45. N. Wales rivers and lakes. S., B/T and sea trout.
46. Eyebrook Reservoir (Rutland). Trout.
47. Grafham Reservoir (Hunts). B/T and rainbows.
48. Draycote Reservoir (Warwicks). B/T and rainbows.
49. Weirwood Reservoir (Sussex). B/T and rainbows.
50. River Wharfe. B/T, grayling and coarse fish.
51. River Lune. S., B/T, sea trout and coarse fish.
52. Aquatells (Basildon). New sport fishing complex. B/T, R/T and coarse fish.
53. The Ouse (Sussex). Sea trout and gen. coarse.
54. Thames and tribs. Trout in higher reaches, weirpools and tributaries.
55. River Kennet. B/T, grayling and coarse fish.
56. Durham and Northumberland rivers. S., B/T and sea trout. Some coarse fish.
57. Lake District. Some salmon, B/T and char.
58. West Country rivers. Good S., B/T and sea trout.

Publication

Where to Fish, published by Harmsworth Press, 8 Stratton Street, London W.1.

Scotland

There are no river licences as such needed to fish in Scotland. Permission to fish or the buying of a fishing permit gives one the right to engage in the sport. Written permission is necessary before anglers may fish for salmon and sea trout.

Close seasons are as follows:
Trout, October 7th-March 14th (both days inclusive).
Salmon. In Scotland the close seasons for this fish are extremely variable, from river to river, so information must be sought from the local District Board or riparian owner.
Coarse fish, as National close season or local regulations.

▶ 151

Sea fishing areas
1. Shetland Islands. Gen. fishing and huge skate.
2. Orkney Islands. Gen., skate and halibut.
3. Caithness District. Gen. species and halibut.
4. North-East coast. Gen. species.
5. Firth of Forth. Gen. good shorefishing at times.
6. Berwickshire coast. Gen. fishing.
7. Western Islands. Gen. boat and shore. Angling surveys show great promise.
8. Ullapool and surrounding area. Gen. boat fishing and big skate.
9. Galloway. Gen. boat and shore. Good flatfish and tope in summer.
10. Firth of Clyde and Isle of Arran. Good gen. boat fishing. Big cod and haddock.

Coarse fishing areas
11. Loch Lomond. Big pike.
12. Loch Maben. Pk., P., B., Rh., chub and B/T. Free fishing on three lochs.
13. River Tweed. Free fishing for Rh. and grayling on tidal stretches.
14. River Nith. Some coarse fish and grayling, by permit.
15. Loch Ken. Good Pk. and P., also game species.

Game fishing areas
16. Orkney Islands. Free fishing for lake and sea trout. Boats available.
17. Isle of Mull. S., B/T, sea trout at reasonable prices.
18. Grantown-on-Sprey. Famous sporting centre with fishing. S., B/T and sea trout.

19. River Tweed. S., sea trout and grayling. Some free B/T fishing.
20. River Annan. S. and sea trout. Some permits available.
21. River Clyde. Good B/T in upper reaches.
22. River Deveron. S., B/T and sea trout. Very good water with some permits.
23. River Teith. Town water with S., B/T and sea trout. Tickets available.
24. Edinburgh (Water of Leith). Corporation water. Tickets available for B/T.

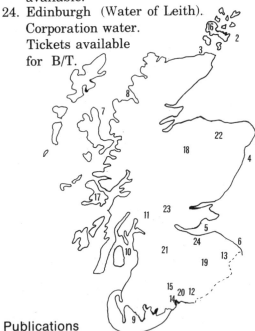

Publications

Where to Fish, published by Harmsworth Press, 8 Stratton Street, London W.1.
Scotland for Fishing, from the Scottish Tourist Board, 2 Rutland Place, Edinburgh 1. Information can also be had from The Scottish Council for Physical Recreation.

Ireland

No rod licence is required to fish for brown trout or coarse species in the Republic of Ireland. A rod licence is necessary when fishing for salmon and sea trout. The country is divided into Districts, each one issuing licences on a weekly or seasonal basis.

In Northern Ireland there are four Fishery Districts, all of which issue licences for salmon or migratory trout. Anyone fishing for brown trout or coarse fish must hold an annual rod licence, but if they fish in water holding salmon and sea trout with tackle capable of catching these species they will also require a salmon licence.

Close seasons are as follows:
Brown trout, February 15th or March 1st—September 30th (some waters close earlier or later—see local regulations). There are minimum size limits in most districts (normally 8 inches).

Salmon fishing areas have widely varying seasons river to river. There is no close season for coarse fish in Eire.

Brown trout fishing is free in many of the large lakes, Corrib, Conn, Mask, Derg, etc. Most private fisheries will issue permits at a moderate cost. The Inland Fisheries Trust, 11 Westmoreland Street, Dublin 2, issues permits for the waters under their control. Free salmon fishing is available in both countries on a few rivers and lakes. Most good waters are in private hands and permits vary in price from 50p per week to £3 per day. Many hotels have salmon and sea trout fishing rights available to guests.

IASCAIREACHT
FISHING

Look for this sign.

Sea fishing areas

1. Kinsale and Cobh. Gen. species and B/shark in summer. Good offshore marks.
2. Ballycotton and Dungarven. Gen., B/shark, bass and mullet.
3. Cahirciveen and Valencia. Good gen. offshore and shark.
4. Dingle Peninsula. Gen. boat fishing, shark, skate and best bass fishing.
5. Clare coast. Gen. boat and shark. Bass from shore marks.
6. Galway Bay and Aran Islands. Gen. boat fishing and porbeagle shark.
7. Westport and Clew Bay. Skate, monkfish and fair shorefishing.
8. Achill Island. Good gen. boat fishing, shark and rock angling.
9. Mullet Peninsula. Good gen. boat fishing, skate and flats.
10. Portrush and Ballycastle. Good gen. fishing. Some bass at times.

Coarse fishing areas.

11. Shannon river systems. B., Pk., P and game species.
12. Cork Blackwater. Rh., dace and game species.
13. L. Conn. Big Pk., P., also game species.
14. Cavan area. Pk., P., B., R. and some trout.
15. L. Corrib and Mask. Pk., P., R. and game species.
16. Lough Erne. Pk., P., R., B., and B/T.
17. Lough Neagh. Eels and coarse fish in shallow waters and feeder streams.
18. Clare Lakes (Ennis). Pk., P., R., T.
19. Lough Melvin area. Large Pk., coarse fish and game species.
20. River Barrow. Pk., P., R., B. and tench. Good trout fishing.

Game fishing areas

21. L. Sheeling, Ennel and lakes around. B/T, Pk, P., and R., except Sheelin.
22. L. Mask. Good B/T.
23. L. Corrib. Big B/T, Pk. and P.
24. L. Derg. Large trout, Pk. and P.
25. River Slaney. Fairly good sea trout in the middle season.
26. R. Blackwater (Cork). S., B/T, sea trout and coarse fish.
27. River Lee. Small trout and salmon in the lower reaches.
28. River Laune and Killarney Lakes. S., B/T and sea trout. Permits available.
29. River Blackwater (Ulster). Good B/T, Pk. and other coarse fish.
30. River Suir. Good B/T fishing. Some free water.

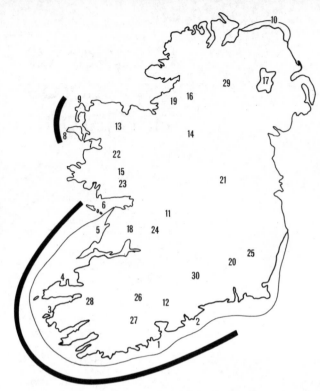

Publications

Brown Trout Fishing
Salmon and Sea Trout Fishing
Coarse Fishing
Sea Angling in Ireland
available from the Irish Tourist Board, Ireland House, New Bond Street, London W.1.
Angling in Northern Ireland
from the Tourist Information Centre, 6 Royal Avenue, Belfast.

The Inland Fisheries Trust also publishes a number of booklets, particularly on fish identification. They also assist in operating the Specimen Fish Award Scheme, in which anglers can submit fish for annual awards.

Chapter 19
Fishing records and jargon

▲ *Freshwater*

Saltwater ▼

154

These freshwater fish are open to claims at the listed minimum qualifying weights.

Bream, silver	2 lbs.
Chub	7 lbs. 8 ozs.
Grayling	4 lbs.
Pike	41 lbs.
Trout, sea	20 lbs.

Species	lbs.	ozs.	dms.	Captor and location
Barbel	13	12	0	J. Day, Royalty Fishery, Hampshire
Bleak		3	15½	Master D. Pollard, Staythorpe Power Station
Bream, Bronze	12	14	0	G. Harper, River Stour, Gt. Cornard
Carp	44	0	0	R. Walker, Redmire Pool
Carp, Crucian	4	6	4	P. H. Oliver, from a lake in Surrey
Catfish	43	8	0	R. J. Bray, Wilstone Res., Tring
Dace	1	4	4	J. Gasson, Little Ouse at Thetford
Eel	8	10	0	A Dart, Hunstrete Lake
Gudgeon		4	0	M. Morris, Susworth Roach Ponds
Perch	4	12	0	S. F. Baker, Oulton Broad
Roach	3	14	0	W. Penney, Lambeth Res. and A. Brown, Stamford
Rudd	4	8	0	Rev. E. C. Alston, Thetford
Trout, Brown	18	2	0	K. J. Grant, Loch Garry
Trout, Rainbow	10	0	4	M. Parker, Kings Lynn
Tench	9	1	0	J. Salisbury, Hemingford Grey
Salmon	64	0	0	Miss G. W. Ballantyne, River Tay
Zander	15	5	0	W. G. Chillingworth, Great Ouse Relief Channel
Angler-fish	68	2	0	H. G. T. Legerton, Canvey Island
Bass	18	2	0	F. C. Borley, Felixstowe
Black Bream	6	1	0	F. W. Richards, The Skerries, Devon
Blonde Ray	35	9	0	A. J. Pierce, The Shambles Bank
Blue Shark	218	0	0	N. Sutcliffe, Looe, Cornwall
Bottle-nosed Ray	76	0	0	R. Bulpitt, Needles, Isle of Wight
Brill	16	0	0	A. H. Fisher, Isle of Man
Bull Huss	21	3	0	J. Holmes, Looe, Cornwall
Coalfish	26	2	0	J. Trust, Start Point, Devon
Catfish	9	12	0	A. Millar, Stonehaven
Cod	46	0	8	R. Baird, Firth of Clyde, Scotland
Common Skate	226	8	0	R. S. Macpherson, Duny Voe, Shetland Isles
Conger Eel	92	13	0	P. H. Ascott, Torquay, Devon
Cuckoo Ray	5	0	0	N. C. McLean, Isle of Arran
Dab	2	10	12	A. B. Hare, The Skerries, Devon
Electric Ray	52	0	0	K. Sprague, Exmouth, Devon
Flounder	5	11	8	A. G. L. Cobbledick, Fowey, Cornwall
Garfish	2	9	2	A. W. Bodfield, Dartmouth

Species	st	lb	oz	Angler, Location
Gurnard, Grey	1	6	0	K. Manson, Brassay, Shetland Isles
Gurnard, Red	3	2	0	W. S. Blunn, off Plymouth
Gurnard, Tub	11	7	4	C. W. King, Wallasey, Cheshire
Haddock	9	4	8	Mrs. L. Morley, Mevagissey, Cornwall
Hake	25	5	8	H. W. Steel, Belfast Lough
Halibut	161	12	0	W. E. Knight, Stromness, Orkney Isles
John Dory	10	12	0	B. L. Perry, Porthallow
Lemon Sole	2	2	15	Master D. Duke, Douglas, Isle of Man
Lssr. Spotted Dogfish	4	8	0	J. Beattie, Ayr, Scotland
Ling	45	0	0	H. C. Nicholl, Penzance, Cornwall
Lumpsucker	14	3	0	W. J. Burgess, Felixstowe, Suffolk
Mackerel	5	6	8	S. Beasley, Eddystone
Mako Shark	500	0	0	Mrs. Joyce Yallop, Eddystone
Monkfish	66	0	0	C. G. Chalk, Shoreham
Mullet, Grey	10	1	0	P. C. Libby, Portland, Dorset
Mullet, Red	3	10	0	J. E. Martel, Guernsey, Channel Isles
Plaice	7	15	0	I. B. Brodie, Salcombe, Devon
Pollack	23	8	0	G. Bartholomew, Newquay
Porbeagle Shark	430	0	0	D. Bougourd, Jersey, Channel Isles
Pouting	5	8	0	R. S. Armstrong, off Berry Head, Devon
Ray's Bream	7	15	12	G. Walker, Hartlepool
Red Bream	7	8	0	A. F. Bell, Fowey, Cornwall
Sandy Ray	5	10	8	J. Boyd, Gourock, Scotland
Scad (Horse Mackerel)	3	4	8	D. Cooke, off The Mewstone, Plymouth
Small-eyed Ray	13	11	8	H. Pout, Bolt Tail
Smooth Hound	28	0	0	A. T. Chivers, Heacham
Sole	4	1	14	R. A. Austin, Guernsey, Channel Isles
Spotted Ray	16	3	0	E. Lockwood, Lerwick, Shetland Isles
Spurdog	17	1	0	S. Bates, off Deal, Kent
Sting Ray	59	0	0	J. M. Buckley, Clacton, Essex
Thornback Ray	38	0	0	J. Patterson, Rustington
Thresher Shark	280	0	0	H. A. Kelly, Dungeness
Tope	74	11	0	A. B. Harries, Caldy Island, S. Wales
Tunny	851	0	0	L. Mitchell Henry, off Whitby, Yorkshire
Turbot	29	0	0	G. M. W. Garnsey, off The Manacles, Falmouth
Undulate Ray	19	6	3	L. R. Le Page, Herm, Channel Isles
Whiting	6	3	3½	Mrs. R. Barrett, off Rame Head, Cornwall
Wrasse, Ballan	7	10	15	B. K. Lawrence, Cornwall

At the time of preparation and going to press, there were several record claims awaiting ratification. For this reason this list has been abridged.

Compiled from the British (Rod-Caught) Fish Committee's list.

How to claim a record

First telephone the Secretary of the British (Rod-Caught) Record Fish Committee, 17 Queen Street, Peterborough, Northants. Telephone Peterborough 4084. Follow this call with a letter setting out the weight, description of species, date and time of capture and method of taking. Give the names and addresses of two witnesses to the capture and the address of the scales on which the fish was weighed. Avoid the use of spring balances, they are often unreliable. Weigh the fish on scales which can later be tested for accuracy. The fish must be retained, by the captor, for inspection.

Fish caught in Ireland should be reported to the Irish Specimen Fish Committee, 11 Westmoreland Street, Dublin 2, Eire. A similar method of claiming operates in that country. 155

Jargon

Anal fin The rearmost fin on the underside of a fish, nearest the tail.

Action The type and amount of bend in a rod, under pressure of casting or playing a fish.

Blank day When no fish are caught.

Bite A fish taking the bait.

Bite indicators Tackle items intended to show that a fish is taking the bait.

B/S or Breaking Strain The measured pull at which a dry line will snap. This measurement differs when the line is wet or has been knotted.

Bung A large, round cork float used when pike fishing.

Butt The handle section of a fishing rod.

Caudle fin The tail fin of a fish.

Cast The throwing out of the end tackle or a length of nylon to which is attached flies or hooks.

Centre-pin reel A revolving drum rotating on a fixed spindle. The handles are fixed on to the reel drum.

Check A ratchet device to prevent line from peeling off the reel too easily; it also gives audible indication of a bite.

Close season A time in which anglers cannot fish for a particular species.

Disgorger An instrument for removal of hooks from the mouths of fish.

Dorsal fin A fin or group of fins on the backs of fish.

Eye The ring on a hook through which the line is threaded and tied.

Feed, Being on Times at which fish are taking an angler's bait.

Ferrule A metal joint between two rod sections or a small brass tube which is threaded on to wire trace material to secure it.

Fixed-spool reel A casting reel which has a bobbin or drum placed at right angles to the rod. Line is picked-up and wrapped around the spool by a bale arm.

Flake A bread bait, the soft crumb from the inside of a new loaf lightly pinched on to the hook.

Float A device made from wood, cane, cork or quills, used to indicate bites from fish. The float will carry a bait to where fish are feeding, suspending the bait at a set depth.

Gaff A hook, attached to a handle, used to land heavy fish that have been played either to a boat or bankside.

Gape The distance between the shank and point of a fishing hook.

Gentles Another name for maggots.

Ground bait Small particles of food, similar to the hook-bait, used to attract and hold fish in a swim.

Holding fish Keeping them within casting range.

Iron Another name for a hook. The term is used by salmon fishermen.

Jack A small pike.

Keep-net A tube of netting, supported by stiff rings, closed at one end. Used to contain an angler's catch in the water during the fishing period.

Lash or lask A fillet from the side of a bait fish.

Leger To fish the bottom with a lead that holds the bait down in a current.

Lateral line A sensory organ which runs

along the sides of a fish's body.

Lobworm The largest of the worms used as a bait.

Long-trotting A method of fishing in running water where the bait is allowed to travel downstream to the fish.

Match fishing A form of angling where anglers compete against each other to catch fish in a definite amount of time.

Otter A mechanical device which is used to free tackle that has become tangled in an underwater obstruction.

Paternoster A method of fishing a bait, above the bottom, in a fixed position using a lead to tether the tackle.

Pectoral fins Paired fins behind the gill case of a fish.

Pick-up The ball arm of a fixed-spool reel. It is opened to cast but when the reel handle is turned will snap over and begin to retrieve line on to the bobbin.

Pirk Artificial lure made in lead or other heavy metal with one treble hook. It is fished jigged up and down.

Plug An imitation fish that is cast out and retrieved the action of which simulates a live creature.

Plummet Used to measure the depth of water in the swim. Made as a lead with a cork insert, to attach to the hook.

Rubby dubby Bag of mashed scraps of fish lowered into the sea from a boat to attract fish.

Sink and draw A technique where the bait is dropped to the bottom, then raised and lowered repeatedly with a fluttering action to attract feeding fish.

Snap tackle Two treble hooks joined by a wire trace for fishing a live or dead fish to catch pike.

Spigot A modern method of joining sections of a glass rod together.

Spinning Casting and retrieving a lure to catch predatory species.

Split shot Lead weights that are sliced so that they may be pinched on to the line to sink a float.

Spoon A type of spinning lure.

Strike The flick or raising of the rod tip which will hook a fish.

Swim The stretch of water in which the angler is fishing, or an area of water where fish are known to lie.

Swim-feeder A hollow container used to carry particles of groundbait to a definite place on the bottom of a lake or river.

Swing tip A type of bite indicator attached to the top section of the rod.

Swivel A metal device which is intended to prevent twist in the line. It has an eye at each end for the attachment of nylon line.

Threadline reel An old-fashioned term for the fixed-spool reel.

Trot To let the float swim freely downstream of the rod.

Treble hook Three hooks joined together to a common eye, used on most spinning baits.

Ventral fins They are paired fins, usually behind the pectorals, sometimes called pelvic fins.

157

Chapter 20
Angling:
the future?

CONDUCTED by the National Anglers' Council, a recent survey shows that there are at least three million anglers in Great Britain. The number is growing annually, with sea and game fishing rapidly catching coarse fishing in popularity. More anglers travel to distant waters than ever before. Some because of crowded local fishing areas but many who find that they have an increase in their leisure hours and more money to spend on following the sport.

It is difficult to forecast the shape of angling in the future, but several trends are becoming noticeable. Increasing numbers of fishermen are joining clubs, no doubt to gain access to more and better fishing. Wealthy clubs are able to use the subscriptions from members to lease and improve waters. They also aid the newcomer to the sport to learn the basic mechanics of fishing in good company. Most clubs and associations arrange a series of winter lectures and film shows. These enable the average angler to learn the techniques that have been, and are constantly being, developed by the leading anglers of this country.

Clubs cater for both the lone fisher, the man that wants to fish alone but joins in the many social functions, and the match or competition angler. This branch of the sport of fishing is growing fast. Apart from open competitions run by the individual clubs there are now a number of commercial organisations that are prepared to sponsor the competitive aspect of fishing. Although this form of angling centres on the catching of small or average size specimens it is highly technical and the exponents of the art of match fishing are extremely skilful. Nevertheless, there will always be a place for the man who wishes to concentrate on catching the big fish. His only problem is to continue to find the sort of environment in which to find the larger-than-average specimens.

If anglers will band themselves together they become a force to whom the people who control our water resources must listen. So much of the available water is in the hands of very few.

It must be remembered that to improve the quality and quantity of the freshwater fishing in this country will cost money. This money can only be found

by charging realistic prices for fishing. It goes without saying that there must be a fair price paid by the angler. In return he must get fair fishing with the possibility of continued improvement in the facilities offered to him. Put-and-take fisheries will succeed for the trout fisherman, as witness the success of the reservoirs that have been established as trout fisheries over the recent years. The coarse fisherman should also expect to be able to fish these public undertakings. Stock new reservoirs on a one-for-one basis. Equal rights for coarse and game anglers.

For the sea fisherman things are different. Until we know just what is going to happen when this country joins the Common Market it is difficult to determine what the trends in the sport will be. We cannot stock the sea in the same way as one can stock fresh water. Certainly areas could be set aside for the sea angler, but it would present enormous problems. Sea anglers are spread right around the coast of the country, so to establish sport fishing areas for the sea angler would mean that people wishing to fish these places would have to travel long distances.

Some thought needs to be given to the construction of offshore habitat of the kind that the Americans are building. They gather old cars, often abandoned here at the roadside, carry them out to a position off the coast and create artificial reefs by dumping them overboard. Naturally they consult the responsible authorities to ensure these man-made

A quiet evening on the river with a fish in the net (far left). *The angler, Jack Shell, hooked this jack pike whilst fishing a worm for chub.*

Tom Ivens, a famed reservoir angler, subdues the wild fight of a rainbow trout. The rod is held high to absorb the last lunges as the fish tries to shed the hook. This rainbow, taken at Draycote Reservoir, is typical of the trout that have been introduced to this man-made lake.

159

fishing grounds are not a hazard to ships. Commercial trawlermen as well as the rod-and-line anglers agree that these reefs can only improve their fishing prospects. For although the reefs become habited by all manner of fish, sooner or later these reef-dwelling fish move out over the flat ground to feed and add to the catches made in the nets.

There is certainly enough rubbish lying around the countryside of this country to create a good number of rod-and-line fishing areas. Shore fishers have blamed pollution for a deterioration in their sport. They are undoubtedly correct in the assumption that inshore fishing is suffering from the effects of all manner of pollutants. To all anglers I would suggest that we all contribute to this worsening situation. Whilst we want our shirts whiter than white our wives will use detergents and other chemicals that cause pollution. If we as a species must use these substances we must also find a way to disperse the harmful effects that they have upon the wildlife of the world. Conservation rarely means stocking or re-introducing species within the ecology. What we must ensure is the conservation of habitat. If the home and living conditions are suitable most species will live, grow and reproduce quite happily without man's interference.

I hope that this book has been of interest to you, that it may have explained some of the reasons for fishing and how we go about it.

Tight lines!

The illustrator. Keith Linsell is concerned with the accurate identification of fish. Because of his deep interest he has become a fine angling artist and naturalist.

The author. Michael Prichard is a photo-journalist and film maker. He specialises in the study of outdoor subjects, animals in the wild and observation of the behaviour of wild creatures.

The end of a successful sea-fishing day.

GONE FISHING

by Michael Prichard

Illustrated by Keith Linsell

Woolworth Leisure Series: Number 1

Published by Daily Mirror Books

50p

First published March 1972

SBN 0 600 33907 6

© 1972 I.P.C. Newspapers Ltd. in association with Michael Prichard and Purnell and Sons Ltd. Published by Daily Mirror Books, 98 St. Pancras Way, Camden, London, N.W.1. Printed by Purnell and Sons Ltd., Paulton, Somerset, and London